AF471158

SPREZZ

THE ART OF EFFORTLESS SUPERIORITY

JANEY PREGER

This book is respectfully dedicated
to the memory of Stephen Potter,
founder of the College of Lifemanship

London

GEORGE ALLEN & UNWIN

Boston   Sydney

**George Allen & Unwin (Publishers) Ltd,
40 Museum Street, London WC1A 1LU, UK**

George Allen & Unwin (Publishers) Ltd,
Park Lane, Hemel Hempstead, Herts HP2 4TE, UK

George Allen & Unwin Australia Pty Ltd,
8 Napier Street, North Sydney, NSW 2060, Australia

George Allen & Unwin with the Port Nicholson Press,
PO Box 11–838 Wellington, New Zealand

First published, 1985

British Library Cataloguing in Publication Data
Preger, Janey
   Sprezz: the art of effortless superiority.
   1. Social interaction — Anecdotes, facetiae,
   satire, etc.
   I. Title
   302'.0207   HM291

ISBN 0-04-827139-X

Set in 11 on 12 point Futura Light by Columns of Reading
and printed in Great Britain by
Anchor Brendon, Tiptree, Essex

SPREZZ

THE ART OF EFFORTLESS SUPERIORITY

JANEY PREGER

This book is dedicated to
the Humpback Whale.
To be hunted to the verge of extinction
is bad enough, but to be deformed as well
is just awful.

London
GEORGE ALLEN & UNWIN
Boston　Sydney

Contents

A note on what you have read so far

If you have persisted with the book to this point, you will have noticed that it has two title pages. The reason for this is very complicated.

It is so that, if you have been given this volume as a present, and the person who bought it for you has inscribed on the title page some such dedication as:

'To Bunny with all my love, Jeremy, Christmas 1985'.

you can remove the disfigured page, using a razor blade or a sharp pair of scissors. You will be left with a book which is apparently intact and can now be offered as a present to someone else.

This is where it gets complicated. Do you, or do you not, remove *this* page as well? If you do, your chicanery should remain undetected. But if you don't, you will be letting the recipient know, in a rather subtle way, that he or she does not rate so highly in your affections as to merit a present that cost money.

Next question: if you in fact *bought* this book to give as a present, should you:

a. leave it intact and unmarked?
b. remove the first title page?
c. remove the first title page and this page as well?
d. remove both title pages but leave this one?
e. inscribe the first title page?
f. inscribe both title pages with identical dedications?
g. write on the first title page a fictitious dedication to yourself, and leave it in?
h. tear out the first title page, write a fictitious dedication to yourself on the second title page, and drop the whole thing in the bath before gift-wrapping it?.

Not sure?
Perhaps you'd better read on.

Introduction

What is *sprezzatura*?

The concept of **hip cool**, of **hanging loose to freak the punters**, was invented in fifteenth-century Italy. Sprezzatura, according to Baldessare Castiglione (1478–1529), was the hallmark of the ideal courtier, a combination of nonchalance and brilliance. It was the effortless technique of the supreme artist, the art that concealed art.

When the Pope was thinking of commissioning Giotto to paint for him, he asked for a demonstration of the artist's skill. Giotto took his pencil and drew a perfect circle. That was sprezzatura.

From renaissance Italy, sprezz spread. Along with slashed doublets and striped tights it became fashionable throughout Europe. In particular, the English took to sprezz in a big way. It appealed to that deep strain in the national character which is compounded of phlegmatic understatement and profound conceit. Drake's 'Plenty of time to finish the game and beat the Spaniards too' was pure sprezz (although, of course, if the Armada had won it would not have been sprezz, it would have been stupid).

The incarnation of English sprezz was Drake's contemporary, Sir Philip Sidney (1554–86). Some of his sprezzier achievements included the following:

Although Sidney failed to take his degree, his Oxford tutor left directions that the fact that this young man had been his pupil should be recorded on his tombstone. Eat your hearts out all you double firsts.

He carried on an affair with Lady Penelope, daughter of the Earl of Essex, addressing to her brilliant but effortless sonnets, in spite of her marriage to Lord Rich and his own marriage to Walsingham's 14-year-old daughter.

Outnumbered in a cavalry battle and shot in the leg, Sir Philip handed his water bottle to a common soldier with the words, 'Thy necessity is yet greater than mine.' This line has gone on to become an all-time sprezz classic.

On his deathbed Sidney improvised a poem *in French*. He had it set to music and got a minstrel to sing it to him while he died. Impressive.

He left so many debts that his funeral was postponed for four months while friends organised a whip-round to pay for it. Such nonchalance! Such sprezz!

The development of British sprezz was set back during the seventeenth century by the victory of the wrong side in the Civil War. It was now apparent that the effortlessly superior cavaliers were not quite able to hold the pose when assaulted by their unashamedly hardworking inferiors, the Roundheads.[1] Thus was born the concept of grace in defeat which has since proved so very useful.[2]

Our last truly sprezzy king, Charles I, went to his execution with the words: 'Let me have a shirt on more than ordinary, by reason the season is so sharp as may probably make me shake, which some observers will imagine proceeds from fear. I would have no such imputation.' (These words have often been misunderstood. The sprezz ploy is not the wearing of an extra shirt, it is the *request* for an extra shirt. The aim was to impress the jailer, not the populace. Once this is grasped it can be seen that the fundamental rule, 'Never acknowledge a sprezz ploy', was not in fact violated in this case.) Attempts to revive this classic ploy have been frustrated in recent years by a scarcity of public executions in Britain, but it is believed to be in regular use in parts of the Middle East to this day.

From the middle of the seventeenth century, the ideal of effortless superiority came to be pursued in specialised

---

[1] The most recent historical parallel, very similar in terms of attitudes and hairstyles, was the assault on the bedraggled remnants of the hippie movement ('stay cool, be beautiful') by the emergent skinheads ('stick the boot in') in the years 1969–71. In both cases survivors took refuge in oak trees ('Plant an acorn for peace' – John Lennon).

[2] The Romans originally developed the concept, of course, but mainly for non-Romans.

ways rather than across the board.[1] The renaissance gentleman, adept in all the arts from warfare to womanising and from poetry to politics, was unable to compete in the end with the single-minded pursuit of excellence in any one sphere of achievement. Sir Francis Bacon (1561–1626) was the last man in Europe of whom it could be said that he knew everything worth knowing. As the world grew more complicated it became clear that superiority in any contest was in practice unlikely to be truly effortless. The transition has been marked by the shift in the meaning of the word 'amateur', which was originally (and in the context of sport remained until very recently) a term of praise: 'One who does it for love rather than money.' Now it means, 'One who isn't good enough to command a fee; one who would not stack up well against Bodie and Doyle; a klutz.'

Despite this shift in public sensibility, the notion of sprezzatura retained its appeal and survived in two distinct historical forms which, for the sake of giving them labels, we may call the *rake* and the *gunfighter*.

The rake behaves in a way we would all love to emulate, but wouldn't dare, and gets away with it. Take for example John Wilmot, the 2nd Earl of Rochester (1647–80), courtier, poet and libertine. The *Dictionary of National Biography* notes with clenched teeth that 'he lacked all sense of shame and rebuffs had no meaning for him'. It quotes the incident when Rochester tried to steal a kiss from the Duchess of Cleveland, she knocked him flat on his back, and he jumped up and recited an impromptu compliment.

Rochester, who once remarked that he had been continuously drunk for five years, was particularly skilled in that variant of basic sprezz which concerns the art of *getting away with things*. He got away with insulting the King ('who never said a foolish thing, nor ever did a wise one') and with kidnapping his intended bride.[2] For the

---

[1] T. S. Eliot's theory of the dissociation of sensibility may be relevant here. Or not.

[2] The ambiguity of this sentence – do I mean the King's intended bride or do I mean Rochester's? – is classic sprezz. When the misunderstanding would be more impressive than the truth, promote the misunderstanding.

latter offence he was, it is true, sent to the Tower, but he was swiftly pardoned and released, and went on to marry the lady, who happened to be rather rich.

With his pal, the Duke of Buckingham, he once took over an inn on the road to Newmarket and the two aristocrats, posing as tavern-keepers, 'conspired to corrupt all the respectable women of the neighbourhood'.

Best of all, he made a classic deathbed repentance, ordered all his indecent poems burned (of course, they weren't) and in the opinion of all concerned went straight to Heaven.

In the pages that follow I shall give practical advice on how to apply the concept of sprezzatura to every aspect of your life. Originally sprezzatura was a fusion of the attributes of effortlessness and superiority. In the centuries since it has become harder and harder to combine the two in a single pose. At some times and in some places it will be judicious to plump for lack of effort and pay the price of some slight loss of superiority. (For example, the student who cannot be sure of getting a first without really trying should always settle for a 'fun third' rather than be seen to *work* for a first.) At other times, in other places, it will be sensible to exert yourself to acquire the superiority which you will subsequently unleash upon the world with a light laugh and a shrug of the shoulders. (For example, it is worth the effort it takes systematically to memorise all the two- and three-letter words in the dictionary, if the result is that you will win at Scrabble *every time*.)

To live your life with minimum effort and maximum enjoyment is to tend to the tradition of the rake. To concentrate on superiority at all costs (however discreetly attained, however elegantly enforced) is to be a gun-fighter. But it is no accident that the most powerful mythic figures in our culture[1] represent that fusion of rake and gunfighter which is the essence of sprezz.

---

[1] Whom I take to be Winston Churchill, Jeeves, the Sundance Kid, George Best in his prime, Douglas Bader, Bette Midler, Rupert Bear, Chuck Berry and Joanna Lumley, not necessarily in that order.

If the sprezzperson is to become
involved in April Fool jokes at all,
they should be memorable ones.

1
SOCIAL STATUS AND THE MYTH OF CLASS SUPERIORITY

To establish oneself in the world one has to do all one can to appear established.
La Rochefoucauld[1]

As a token of my intention to be entirely open and frank about the techniques of sprezz (techniques which are usually hidden and, as the CIA puts it, totally deniable), I shall begin by admitting that the purpose of this opening paragraph of chapter 1 is to separate the opening quote above from the opening footnote below. It has no other function.

---

[1] This quotation was originally delivered in French. By translating it for you I have irritatingly suggested that I have little regard for your linguistic scholarship.

The rules governing the sprezz use of aphorisms, quotations and plagiarism in general may as well be learned now. If you should ever come out with a remark in conversation which sounds as though it might be a quotation from somebody famous (and you will, Oscar, you will) you must attribute it, using some such phrase as 'I think it was Emily Dickinson who said . . .' or 'to quote Dr Johnson . . .' It is no good at all kicking off with 'Who was it who said . . .?' or 'I once read somewhere that . . .' Your opponent will only supply the attribution (and even in some cases correct the wording) leaving you looking foolish.

No, you must ascribe your *bon mot* to a source. Any source is better than none, but obviously some sources are better than others, as Robert Carrier used to say. And the more precise your attribution the better.

Similarly, this second paragraph is here to keep the main text going while the extended footnote, continued from the previous page, burbles away underneath. I would, however, take the opportunity to remark that the main purpose of footnotes in academic works is to provide a spurious patina of impressive scholarship, while freeing the writer from any obligation to present ideas in an orderly sequence.

It is a vulgar assumption of our time that social superiority can be attained only by being either well born

---

(Footnote continued.)

Don't say, '"Pour out the wine without restraint or stay," as it says in the Bible.' Rather say: '"Pour out the wine without restraint or stay." Isaiah seventeen verse three.' If your opponent challenges the attribution thus: 'Surely that's a quote from Spenser?' You reply: '. . . who, of course, took it from Isaiah.' Or even: 'No, actually, but it sounds ever so like him, doesn't it?' (The line is, need I say, from Spenser's *Epithalamion*). Field tests have shown that a confident ascription will be publicly challenged, *even by someone who knows it's wrong*, on only one occasion in twenty-four. So feel free to ascribe your half-remembered quotes to whichever source seems most appropriate. But use this freedom responsibly. For example, do not ascribe a line to Shakespeare when it can plausibly be given to Beaumont and Fletcher, or to Wogan when it might have been Wolfman Jack. Other OK ascriptions are: Lao Tzŭ (or anyone else with a funny little squiggle attached to the spelling of their name), Flaubert (in preference to Dickens), Keith Richard or John Lennon (but not Mick Jagger, Paul McCartney or, God forbid, Ringo), Valerie Solanas (for all the bits of Germaine Greer you half-remember), Bakunin (rather than Marx or Lenin), Henry Thoreau, Stephen Leacock, the Upanishads (especially the lesser-known ones), Verlaine, Spinoza, H. L. Mencken, Hughie Green and Joe Mankiewicz (but on no account Proust, Clive James, Sam Goldwyn, Marshall McLuhan, Peter Fiddick, Bob Dylan, Dylan Thomas or Dylan the rabbit out of 'Magic Roundabout').

If you are planning to introduce a new line into the act, do first establish that it has not been republished recently by Jilly Cooper, Kenneth Williams, Ned Sherrin, Robert Morley, Nigel Rees, etc. No need to check them all; if any three of the better-known snappers-up of carefully-considered trifles have failed to use it, you are probably OK.

or very rich. This is the merest snobbery, and it is believed only because the middle classes tend to be both insecure about their origins and extremely greedy. Of course, anyone with the 'right' accent, the 'right' friends and the 'right' clothes can make other people feel inferior, and nothing is to be done about that. But these things are not sprezzatura, they are only substitutes for it. Those who have the real thing don't need to be aristocrats or millionaires. They need only the intelligence and confidence to make the best use of what they've got.

The woman who is naturally beautiful wins every time against the woman who flogs herself through aerobics classes and beauty regimes in pursuit of the ideal, but both of them can be defeated by the woman who can make her friends and lovers truly believe that looks don't matter.

The ace, king and queen of breeding, wealth and success can be trumped by the two, three and four of sprezz.[1] So your aim in life should not be to drive a Lamborghini (unless you genuinely want to drive at 180 miles an hour). It should be to make the Lamborghini owner wish, in a sudden flood of self-disgust, that he (or she) could be more like you, even if it meant driving around in a second-hand Capri. This is difficult but not impossible. Ask yourself this: why is that person driving a car like that in the first place if not because of some deep sense of insecurity? And where there is insecurity in the opponent, however slight, however well-concealed, sprezz can go to work. With a little sprezz, a dustman can flummox a duchess. Or to put it another way: **With a little sprezz, a dustman can flummox a duchess**.

The first advantage of sprezz, then, is that it requires no great good fortune or hard work in the birth or money departments.[2] The second advantage is that it is infinitely adaptable. An aristocrat knows how to impress only

---

[1] Throughout this book, certain sentences will be in bold type. This is done mainly for effect, but also to help future compilers of books of quotations who may not have time to read the whole thing.

[2] See the forthcoming Sprezzatura Enterprises publication, *How to Drive a Sloane Ranger Tonto.*

those who are impressed by aristocracy. A millionaire can bask and preen only in the company of those whose tongues hang out for cash in bulk. But effortless superiority is a relative term. It doesn't mean superiority to everyone all the time; it means superiority in whatever place, among whatever people, you happen to be at any given moment. The well-judged sprezz ploy is tailored precisely to the circumstances in which it is used. It is selected to suit the audience.[1]

For example, if you are seeking to impress your neighbours, you don't have to make them think you live in a stately home. They know where you live, and it's not that amazing. All you require is that they should feel properly embarrassed about their own accommodation every time they look at yours. On the other hand, if you want to impress people who don't know where you live, and are unlikely ever to visit your home, you have more latitude for a variety of possible approaches. You can contrive to suggest that your domestic circumstances are anything from Brideshead Been-there-all-along (a vague reference to the woodworm in the beams of the great hall) to a cardboard box under Charing Cross Bridge (the 'knife-in-the-middle-class-guilt' approach).

An intellectual audience will be impressed by your detailed knowledge of post-war Balkan poetry ('I suppose, in his way, Miroslav Holub is as interesting as Ivan Lalič'), whereas an audience of hearty rugger players will not begin to look pale and thoughtful until they have heard your amusing tale of the scrum-half who 'accidentally' gouged his eye out on the protruding end of your broken collar-bone.[2]

It begins to look as though I am demanding too much of my reader. Surely it is unrealistic to expect that you can adjust your appearance, manners, accent and conversa-

---

[1] 'Audience' in this context means those inferior to you who don't yet realise it but soon will.

[2] These are 'basic sprezz' ploys. Advanced sprezz goes a stage further and impresses the intellectuals with the eye-gouging (this is known as Mailerism) and the rugger set with the poetry ('Real courage is a lonely thing, don't you think?'). But this is to get ahead of ourselves.

tion to impress absolutely any sort of person? Well, yes. You're quite right. It can't be done.[1] The best you can hope for is to operate effectively across a wider social range than most other people. But here there is a difficulty and it has to do with class.

Like the Hindu, the Briton can derive his self-respect, when all else fails, from his marks of caste. Unless you can undermine this last and most daunting line of defence, you will not make him grovel. And if his class happens to be 'higher' than yours, or if he believes that it is, your task is daunting indeed.

You will never solve the problem by getting hold of a lot of money and spending it on a Rolls Royce, a manor house and a course of elocution lessons. Nor will you manage it by mugging up your Nancy Mitford and teaching yourself to say lavatory, writing paper and looking-glass instead of toilet, notepaper and mirror. A phoney upper-class act cobbled together by studying the *Tatler* and memorising debutantes' nicknames will last all of two minutes before someone asks you whether you know 'Boofy' and you say you were at school with her brother and then realise they're talking about a French painter. Don't do it.

No, the solution is in your own mind. It lies in the realisation that everyone is insecure about class. The more assiduously people reinforce the class barriers around themselves, the more insecurity they betray. To complicate matters, each class has its own particular little worries. If you know what these are — if you can put a finger on the nerve centre, as it were — you can win against any class of opposition.

The working class worries about money. Of course, all classes worry about money, but the difference is that the working class thinks money confers status. At this level, class equals flash, and you score points not so much for having money as for chucking it about. One of the cheapest dashes you'll ever cut in an East End pub is 'accidentally' to drop a five pound note and then leave it

---

[1] Study this technique of argument. It is called the Disarming Admission.

on the floor because you can't be bothered to bend down and retrieve it.

The lower-middle class has two major worries: education and employment. You can dress like an Arkansas share-cropper, drive a five-year-old Datsun Cherry, talk (and smell) like Henry Cooper, and pick your nose, but if your LMC adversary thinks either that you are Eton and Oxford *or* that you have an impressive (not necessarily well-paid) job, you will be deferred to in a manner sometimes verging on the sickening.

Moving into the middle-middle to upper-middle range, we encounter that nebulous concept, 'lifestyle'. Originally upper-mid when it was first formulated in the early sixties, the notion of lifestyle is moving steadily downmarket, leaving – and this is where your opportunity lies – a bit of a vacuum at the upper end of the range. When one uses the word one alludes to such adjectives as 'executive', 'fast-moving', 'trendy' and 'casual'. Stretching from A for Acorn computer to Z for zebra-striped duvet, the lexicon of lifestyle is holy writ to those who think *making it* is a matter of consumer durables and interior design. Another word for this is 'coloursupp'. In fact 'coloursupp' is the term sprezzy people prefer to use, as in:

'What do you think of the new curtains?'

'Very coloursupp.'

'Oh.'

But remember always that nothing dates faster than the latest thing. Even the word 'modern' has an old-fashioned sound to it these days. The upper-mids are starting to realise this, and grope around for a 'lifestyle' they sometimes call 'contemporary classic'. Do not be deceived. It means Habitat 1976 and who the hell can afford to redecorate every six months? They are desperately vulnerable.

The point that has to be made forcefully and repeatedly to the twitchy acolytes of *Homes and Gardens* is that taste is not available through mail order. Wit, originality, learning and savoir-faire are not purchasable commodities. Any putdown which turns upon this fact will do nicely for the mid-to-uppers. A couple of classic examples will illustrate the point:

'They're the sort of people who have to buy their own silver.' (i.e. They have no breeding.)

The Hon. Mrs Nellie Levy, when someone admired her necklace: 'But my dear, these are my gardening pearls.' (i.e. 'You have no taste.')

Edith Evans, on being told that Nancy Mitford was borrowing a friend's villa in the south of France to finish a book: 'Oh really? What's she reading?' (i.e. 'Lifestyle? Don't talk to me about lifestyle!')

The lifestyle putdown drives home the fact that what your adversary thinks gives him class, you know to be irrelevant (because you are higher class than he knows how to be). That's why an aristocrat would tend to despise anyone who drives a brand new Mercedes – 'the sort of car', as Paul Fussell puts it in his book on the American class system, 'owned by Beverly Hills dentists or African cabinet ministers'.

And what worries the aristocracy? It seems that the highest stratum of society is split between those who worry about the obligations imposed by their exalted status ('noblesse oblige') and those who wish they could have more fun. Your first task, then, is to determine which sort of aristo you're dealing with. After that, it's simply a matter of choosing from the appropriate range of tried-and-tested sprezz-ploys. Confronted by a Type A upper, try this one:

Sprezzperson	I see the vicar's asking for money again. Dry rot in the choir-stalls. I suppose one has a duty to pitch in.
Type A	I suppose so. Do you think it's a cheque-book job or a hamper for the Church Garden Party?
Sprezzperson	I'd have said a cheque. But then, oughtn't one to be devoting all one's efforts to the Third World charities? Oxfam and whatnot?
Type A	Oh one does that as well, of course. One gives what one can.
Sprezzperson	I'm not talking about giving money. That's easy. I'm talking about giving one's time. Getting *involved*.

Type A	Well yes, I suppose one should. I do feel rather guilty.
Sprezzperson	And yet, on the other hand, one feels one has a special responsibility to support the arts. Opera . . . ballet . . . they desperately need patronage.
Type A	You're right. And, of course, money isn't enough. One really must get *involved*.
Sprezzperson	Mind you, the last thing Covent Garden needs is some well-meaning busybody trying to interfere.
Type A	Quite. Perhaps a straightforward donation . . .
Sprezzperson	And then again, does one have any right to spend one's money on opera when the world is starving?
Type A	I suppose not.

(Type A is now hopelessly confused. How *does* one give one's money away without feeling guilty and inadequate about it? You move in for the kill.)

Sprezzperson	So how much shall I tell the vicar to put you down for?
Type A	Erm . . .

None of this cuts any ice at all with Type B, who probably represents the larger slice of the upper crust. Type B feels no guilt about owning racehorses, yachts, Learjets and newspapers. In this gossip-column world, the name of the game is glitter. We're back where we started: class equals flash and if you've got it, flaunt it.

However, as any reader of the Sunday tabloids will tell you, There-Is-A-Lot-Of-Unhappiness-Among-The-Rich. Dimly realising that the caviare 'n' champagne life is Somehow Hollow, your Type B flounces and fornicates his way through the social whirl with a growing sense of desperation. Surely there must be more to Having Fun than this? Enter Sprezzperson:

Sprezzperson	Having fun?
Type B	Oh, yes. Super.
Sprezzperson	Really? I mean, in an ideal world, is this really what you'd choose to be doing?
Type B	Well I don't know. It's quite nice . . .
Sprezzperson	I must say, the things *I* really enjoy doing are things one doesn't normally do at all. For example, have you ever stood on the terraces and watched a football match?
Type B	Well no . . .
Sprezzperson	Have you ever spent a whole evening in a perfectly ordinary pub, picked someone up and had a snog in a bus-shelter on the way home?
Type B	Well no actually . . .
Sprezzperson	Tell me, have you ever committed a burglary, just to see what it's like?
Type B	Of course not.
Sprezzperson	(Looking round at the assembled company) You know, I sometimes think that people like these don't know what *real* living is! (Long pause)
Type B	Look here, how does one get tickets for a football match?

It is not an original observation that[1] the aristocracy has more in common with the working class than either has with the great mass of middles in between. After all, there were lords and peasants long before there were trades-men and usurers. Take the question of relations (or, as the lower-middles call them, relatives). Both uppers and

---

[1] This is an excellent way to start a sentence. Write it down.

lowers are family-oriented; they spend a lot of time in the company of parents, grandparents, aunts, uncles, cousins and in-laws. The middle classes, by contrast, take the Oscar Wilde view: 'Relations are simply a tedious pack of people who haven't got the remotest knowledge of how to live nor the smallest instinct about when to die.' They tend, in short, to be ashamed of their families (often with good reason). You can *use* this.

Sprezzperson	We're having a little dinner party on the fifteenth. Perhaps you and Mark would like to come?
Middle-class Victim	Oh yes, we'd love to.[1]
Sprezzperson	Good. And bring your parents.
MCV	Parents? Mum and Dad? I mean, Mummy and Daddy? Ah. Yes. Well. They've not been awfully well . . .
Sprezzperson	Oh dear, I'm sorry to hear that. Well look, why don't we postpone it until they're feeling better?
MCV	Ah. Erm. Yes. Right. Fine.

Or even

Sprezzperson	I believe you have an aunt in Slough?
MCV	That's right. Auntie Nellie.
Sprezzperson	Well look, we're going to be driving out to Oxford next week. I'd love to stop by and meet her. Do you think you could scribble a note of introduction?
MCV	A note of . . .? Er, yes. All right.
Sprezzperson	I always think people's aunties are marvellous.
MCV	(Doubtfully) Mmm. Terrific.

(The ploy is not, of course, complete until you have been to Slough, visited Auntie Nellie and her seven smelly cats, played three-card brag for a couple of hours, drunk

---

[1] This is in any case the wrong reply. See chapter 6.

several pots of strong tea and stocked up on embarrassing anecdotes about Victim's childhood. Then, when you see Victim again, you are in a position to say:)

Sprezzperson	Isn't Auntie Nellie wonderful?
MCV	Wonderful? I mean, mm, wonderful!
Sprezzperson	Listen, when's she coming to stay with you? We simply *must* take her out to lunch.
MCV	Ah. Well we don't actually . . . I mean . . .
Sprezzperson	Do let us know, anyway. I'm dying to introduce her to the Braithwaites.
MCV	The B-B-Braithwaites?
Sprezzperson	Absolutely. Charlotte breeds cats too, you know.

————————**Name-Dropping**————————

If you have a name to drop (and do be sure it's worth dropping; ask yourself whether you are open to counter-attack with the response '*Who*?') do not chuck it into the conversation at random. Use it for maximum effect. Remember, it is more impressive to avoid using the name until driven to it, and then to give it with great reluctance.

'I can't make it tomorrow. I have to go to the theatre. It's one of those things I can't really get out of . . .

What's the play?

Oh some new effort. I'm only going at all to oblige one of the actors.

Who's that?

Oh just an old mate of mine. He likes me to be there when he does an opening night. Sort of a good luck thing.

Yes, but who is it?

I don't know if I should mention his name. He might not want everyone to know about his little insecurity thing.

I won't tell anyone, I promise.

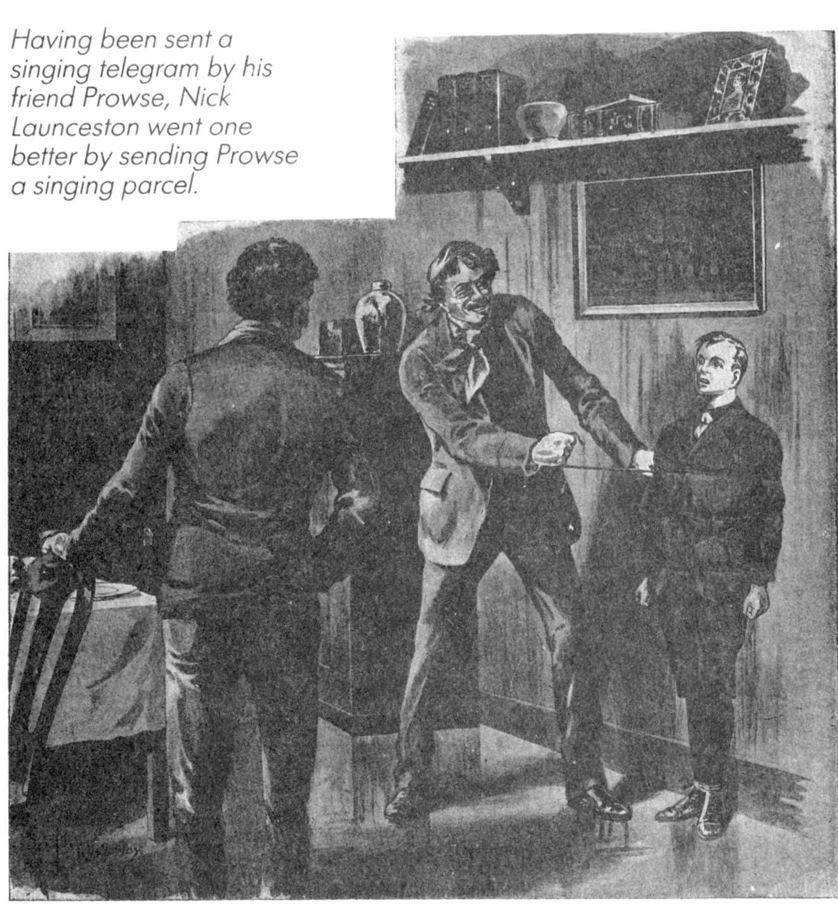

Having been sent a singing telegram by his friend Prowse, Nick Launceston went one better by sending Prowse a singing parcel.

No really, I shouldn't think you'll know him anyway. He's not on telly much.

Who? Who? Come on, who?[1]

Feller named Albie. Albert, he calls himself these days. Albert Finney . . . Odd name for an actor. He's quite good actually.

Never Queue

One of the clearest marks of class superiority is one's refusal to allow oneself to be treated like an ordinary member of the public. This is mainly a matter of attitude, and the test case is the queue.

Lady Hester Cholmondely-ffoote's[2] work in this field has been outstanding. Here are just a few of the ploys she has perfected:

At the bank

When she wishes to cash a cheque, Lady Hester rings the bank and makes an appointment with the manager. Shown into his office, she hands him the cheque with a wordless glare. So far he has not had the nerve to direct her to the cashier's window.

At the doctor's

'My dear, I can't possibly wait. I'm seeing Sir Norman at eleven. He's absolutely determined to operate. Tricky one, apparently. Fifty-fifty chance of success. Anyway, since I had ten minutes in hand, I thought I *must* pop in and see Derek for a second opinion.'

At the taxi rank

Lady Hester approaches the person at the head of the queue with the line:

'Can I offer you a lift John? It is John, isn't it?'
'Frank actually.'

---

[1] There is a school of thought which passionately insists that the name should not be used even at this point. Certainly if you can come up with a knock-down alternative it is to be preferred. We rather like: 'No, I'm sorry, I mustn't say. He's a bit touchy about his privacy. You should have seen what he did to Eamonn Andrews.'

[2] née Tina Satterthwaite.

'Of course. Where are you going?'
'Finchley.'
'Perfect.'

When the taxi arrives:

'Look, driver, can we go to Finchley? But first I want to make a weeny detour to Hampstead.' (Hampstead is five miles in the wrong direction.)

When they get to Hampstead:

'I insist, John, that you allow me to pay the fare.' (She pays what's on the meter and alights, leaving Frank to pay for the journey back to where he started as well as the trip to Finchley.)

In the self-service café

Lady Hester asks for the manager and demands to inspect the kitchens. She consults the chef about recommended dishes, and allows herself to be persuaded to try a little of today's speciality.

'Excellent,' she nods. 'I shall be sitting by the window.'

The food is brought to her table by the manager. She tips exactly 12½ per cent.

Accent

Until the late 1950s, the most impressive accents in British society were variants of the Home Counties public school bray. During the sixties, however, attitudes changed. Certain sorts of working-class and provincial accents became chic, particularly as heard in the mouths of pop stars, photographers, models, trendy playwrights and gangsters. At the same time several of the established upper-class accents, such as the Rattigan cut-glass tinkle and the Indian Army polo-field bray, were mocked to the verge of extinction.

Today, any of the following accents is suitable for the sprezzperson: Liverpool, Cockney (but not Dagenham), pre-war upper (but not Royal family clenched-teeth aristo), Highland or Glasgow (but not Kelvinside and probably not Edinburgh), Southern Irish (only), Boston and Australian.

Non-sprezz accents include Yorkshire, radio disc-jockey, Birmingham, West Country (oo-ar oo-ar), Welsh and French.

All other accents are, in sprezz terms, what you make of them. Especially Geordie.

A word of warning is appropriate here. If you are determined to cultivate a colourful accent, you must also acquire the relevant slang. Too many ersatz Liverpudlians are still drivelling on in nasal tones about scuffers, jiggers, jam butties and judies, unaware that real scousers knocked all that folksy rubbish on the head years ago. Nor will a smattering of East End patois picked up from 'Minder' be sufficient to impress a genuine Cockney, or even anyone who once met one.

The first requirement for the Cockney who seeks to impress is a thorough command of rhyming slang, which is in itself profoundly sprezz. It was invented as a device partly to baffle and exclude outsiders, and partly to promote the image of warm and intimate Cockney camaraderie with which your true eel-guzzling, winkle-gobbling Lambeth pain-in-the-bum likes to torment the rest of us. Problems can arise, however, when two Cockneys try to upstage one another. Take Tel and Samantha, here showing off to a provincial rube called Nigel:

Tel	So there I was, toolin' along the natterjack with me pork an' ham blastin' down me Persians . . .
Nigel	I'm sorry ha ha, I'm afraid you'll have to translate.
Tel	Natterjack toad – road, OK? Persian rugs – lugs – ear'oles, right? Pork an' ham – Sony Walkman. Gorrit?
Samantha	'E reckons 'e's a dab 'and at the ole fruit salad, does our Tel.
Nigel	Fruit salad?
Samantha	Tell 'im what fruit salad is, Tel.
Tel	Erm . . .
Samantha	It's rhyming slang, innit?
Tel *Nigel*	Fruit *salad*?
Samantha	(Making it up as she goes along) Fruit salad rhymes wiv ballad, that's

an ancient folk-song, rhymes wiv
ping-pong, ping-pong's table
tennis, Dennis the Menace, out of
Beano, *Beano*'s a comic, rhymes wiv
atomic, atomic bomb, bombs go
bang, rhymin' *slang*. Y'see?

Nigel	I only know the traditional ones like 'apples and pears'.
Tel	Oh yurr. Apples an' pears – tits. Everyone knows that. 'Ere, I like your centrifugal.
Nigel	Centrifugal?
Tel	Yeah. Centrifugal force – bow tie.
Samantha	That don't rhyme, Tel.
Tel	Well it don't have to rhyme to be good. I mean, look at T. S. Eliot. A lot of his stuff didn't rhyme. Nobody said he wasn't a proper Cockney. Trouble wiv you, darlin', you've got your space invaders up the Pharaoh's daughter wiv the stapling machine round the Pakistani gobble an' chew, y'know?
Samantha	You filthy little Marmite, I'll give you a curtain-rail round the lily-pad.
Tel	Don't you chimney-stack me, you old french-polish. I've rhubarb pie with better downspouts than you . . .
Samantha	Any more of your carbon paper, you little hey-presto, an' I'll ship-in-a-bottle your Trusthouse Fortes . . .

(Nigel leaves quietly at this point.)

Summary

The golden rule of sprezz is: **Be more or be opposite but never be less**. Applying this to the question of class, the sprezzperson should aim to be of a higher class than the opposition, or to be so outrageously declassé as to make the opposition feel uncomfortable. Anything in between is a mistake. [1]

As a general rule, then, if you cannot plausibly purport to be of a higher class, put yourself outside the system altogether. Whatever class you were born into, flout its conventions; trample on its taboos; slaughter its sacred cows. Become a person who evades categorisation, a person to whom labels do not stick. If you are successful, you will join a class of your own, sometimes called the New Bohemians, sometimes described as the Unmonied Aristocracy. If you can't always count on the respect and admiration of those still enmeshed in the traditional class system, you will at least drive them barmy.

---

[1] Note that this rules out 'social climbing', one of the least sprezzy of human activities. The social climber sucks up to class superiors in order to discomfit class equals. Neither group is particularly impressed.

It is extremely unsprezzy, when greeting black people, to go beyond the conventional handshake. The 'gimme five' hand-slapping routine needs a lot of practice, and if inexpertly done can cause offence.

1. You are invited to ride with the local hunt, but you have never ridden anything bigger than a seaside donkey and you know you will fall off as soon as your horse breaks into a canter. Do you reply:

a. 'Sorry, but I've promised to turn out for the Hunt Saboteurs. Perhaps I'll see you there'?

b. 'Sorry, but last time I hunted with your lot some fool tried to follow me over an eight-foot hedge and broke his neck. Led to a bit of a row with the MFH. Called me a mad bugger. I told him where to stick his bugle . . .'?

c. 'I'd love to, but I can't ride a horse. Can I come on a bicycle?'?

2. You owe a dinner invitation to the Coddingtons, whose house is a good deal more impressive than your own down-at-heel semi. Do you:

a. Invite them to join you for a picnic by the river, and hire a Rolls-plus-chauffeur to deliver the Fortnum's hamper?

b. Send them an invitation to dinner with so vague and misleading an address that they'll never find it?

c. Meet them in the pub at closing time and ask everyone in the place back to your house for a Chinese takeaway and a few cans of lager?

3. Your friend, a Fellow of All Souls, asks
    you where you were educated. In fact you
    are an undistinguished graduate of the
    Salford College of Technology. Do you tell
    him:

a. 'I learned everything I know from
    studying tea-towels.'?

b. 'It depends what you mean by education.
    If you take the word in its strict Latin
    sense, the answer is, surprisingly enough,
    Salford.'?

c. 'Privately.'?

4. Wandering into a pub in an unfamiliar
    part of the city, you find yourself the only
    white person among a throng of jolly
    Jamaicans. Some stare, some grin, some
    make jocular remarks. Do you:

a. Ask whether Winston has been in with
    the stuff?

b. Tell them you're researching a Channel
    Four documentary?

c. Inquire politely about the availability of
    break-dancing lessons?

5. Travelling second class by British Rail, you
    meet a couple of friends in the buffet
    queue. They invite you to join them for
    the rest of the journey. Unfortunately,
    however, they are travelling first class. Do
    you say:

a. 'I'm travelling second. I find it induces a
    wonderful sense of existential alienation,
    of the *otherness* of other people, you
    know?'?

b. 'I'm travelling second. I'm doing the
   Trans-Siberian next summer and I thought
   I'd better get in training.'?

c. 'I always travel second and give the
   money I save to Oxfam. It seems such a
   little sacrifice to make.'?

Now check your score

Mostly (a)s You have grasped the principle but need to work harder on your basic arrogance. Ask yourself whether you are sometimes in danger of being over-subtle.

Most (b)s Your natural deviousness is a useful beginning. Sliding out from under a potential put-down is half the battle. But you haven't won until you have put the opposition at a similar disadvantage.

Mostly (c)s Well done. You have in you the seeds of true sprezz-greatness. Nurture them well. Looking at the answers before answering the questions is an admirable habit.

2
Caution, Sprezz at Work

> *It is most important in*
> *this world to be pushing,*
> *but it is fatal to seem so.*
> **Benjamin Jowett**

When Dragoman Hythe delivered his celebrated remark, 'Sprezzatura does not work,' he was not, as many thought at the time, criticising the concept of sprezz. He was simply restating its eternal attitude to the whole question of paid employment.[1]

To understand this, we must look back to the dawn of sprezz, the Renaissance. For the renaissance gentleman the only proper employment was that of *being a gentleman*. Work was not necessarily avoided, but it was done for its own sake rather than for financial reward. One might have a position, a set of duties or even a 'calling', but one would certainly not have a job.

How does this apply to the present? It suggests, I think, a certain *stance vis à vis* employment. In the first place, the sprezzperson may work and may be paid a salary or even a wage, but will always give the impression that this occupation would be pursued for its intrinsic interest and reward even if there were no money in it.

In the second place, the sprezzperson never allows the job to define or condition the personality. The sprezzperson's employment is by no means the most interesting fact about him or her. As V. C. Chamberlain has

---

[1] See my 1982 monograph, *What Dragoman Meant: Sprezzatura in Thatcher's Britain.* Pilchard Press. 138pp.

remarked, 'The cultured person is one who can talk for an hour without revealing his occupation.'[1]

In the third place, whatever the employment may be, the sprezzperson appears to work less but be more successful at it then others in the same occupation.

Jobs are diverse and specialised, so it is difficult to generalise about this area. Perhaps the best way to examine sprezzatura in action in the field of employment is to consider a couple of case histories.

Bulimia Longbotty[2] left school with two O-levels and a certificate for swimming 25 yards. She was also ugly.

She hitch-hiked to Piraeus, where she learned customer-management and portion-control in a Graeco-Chinese restaurant. Such were her obvious abilities that the restaurant proprietors eventually offered her a job. She kept it for six weeks before contracting hepatitis.

Repatriated, thanks to the British Embassy in Athens, Bulimia went into the pornographic video business, starting in a small way by being the person employed on the set to mix the cornflour and water (her training in portion-control here proved invaluable).

It was no coincidence that, soon after employing Bulimia, the Rapallo brothers[3] found themselves subject to increasing police harassment. With all seven brothers in jail, the way was clear for Bulimia (whose relations with the police had always been close) to take over the entire operation.

At this point, however, she suddenly disappeared from public life and might never have been seen again, had not Redwald Pye,[4] a scuba enthusiast from Chelmsford,[5] collided with something spongy in an Essex gravel pit.

Where did Bulimia go wrong?

If she had tried harder at school, she could have emerged with more impressive qualifications. Anyone who can swim 25 yards can surely manage 50. This may

---

[1] Chamberlain was writing in 1952, when persons were male.
[2] Not her real name.
[3] Not the real name of the two youngest.
[4] Not his real name (which was Gordon Wilch).
[5] Actually Ongar.

not sound terribly important, but towards the end it could have made all the difference.

If you have all of Europe to choose from, Piraeus is a bad place to start. Try one of the inner suburbs of Rotterdam. Or Valladolid.

Any list of the employers you should at all costs avoid would have to include Greeks, Chinese, restaurateurs and brothers whose names end in 'o'.

The hepatitis was a sound move. Nothing to criticise there.

Educational and training videos are not only more respectable than porn, they are also a more lucrative racket.

If you are going to stab your employers in the back, you should avoid being identified as the cause of their misfortune. In Bulimia's case, a brief prison sentence of her own (perhaps as accessory after the fact) might have helped.

Overall, Bulimia's career illustrates the futility of trying to start at the bottom and work your way up.

Let us turn to a success story – Byron Peel.[1]

Like Bulimia, Byron was academically undistinguished. He never even learned to swim. Between the ages of 16 and 23 he did little but drink lager and watch television.

One Monday evening, having viewed a particularly unsatisfying episode of a series about American detectives in cars with bald tyres, he picked up the telephone:

'International directory inquiries please. I'd like the number for Plinn-Wacker Productions, Los Angeles.

Thank you.

Hello. Is that Plinn-Wacker Productions?
Write this down. London 292–6191. OK, lemme talk to your market research guy, whatsisname?

Brad Foodman, yeah.

Brad? Byron. Listen, I caught Pudding and Crutch or whatever the hell you call it. It's showing in Europe.

---

[1] Someone else's real name.

Yeah, I'm in England.

Thing is, Brad, I figure you need help. You're slipping.
The format – people must have told you this – is tired.
I mean somnolent, yeah? Let me have two months and a
coupla hundred . . .
coupla hundred *grand* dummy . . . an' I verbally guarantee
I can turn it around for ya. I'm not talking computers.
I'm not talking sample audiences. You can get hung up
on demographics. I'm talking old-fashioned gut reaction.
How about it? No? Well, up yours meathead.'

(SLAMS DOWN PHONE. THREE MINUTES LATER IT
RINGS)

'Brad? Don't apologise. Just tell your people to fix the
flight and I'll see you Thursday. You've got my number.
Oh, and fire the continuity girl. Do it now, while you
remember . . .'

(CLICK)

Byron spent six weeks in Hollywood and came home with
a suntan and enough money to launch a modest dry-
cleaning business which he operates to this day.[1]

Moral: don't be too greedy. Half a million is too much to
ask from a complete stranger.

———————— **Choosing a Career** ————

'Work is a form of nervousness' – Don Herold.

Most young people, when considering a possible career,
ask themselves three questions:
    What job am I qualified to do?
    What job will I enjoy?
    What job will eventually make me rich?
    This is the right number of questions, but they are the
wrong questions. Here are the questions they ought to
ask:

---

[1] 10 February 1985.

What job will be easy to do?

What job sounds more impressive than it actually is?

How much will it matter if I turn out to be lousy at it?

A casual glance at the labour market reveals that an easy, impressive-sounding job in which it is difficult to measure success or failure will also tend to be both lucrative and enjoyable. In fact whole occupations are based on people getting a lot of money for doing little or no work. Such people call themselves 'consultants', 'agents', 'advisers', 'supervisors', 'visualisers', 'garage mechanics', 'dons', 'solicitors', etc. Their jobs consist of seeming busy, rather than actually working.

For those who consider this analysis excessively cynical, sprezzmistress Violet Teithe[1] has written helpfully on the subject of sprezzatura and careers.[2] She divides employment into classes of desirability, as follows:

Class One

No visible means of support. This can be impressive at almost any income level (see chapter 1).

Class Two

Other people's hobbies. You are able to make a living out of an activity which others do for fun, e.g. carpenter, photographer, cook, writer, gambler, painter, actor, prostitute.

Class Three

Worthwhile employment. You can plausibly claim that your job is fulfilling and/or important, e.g. teacher, politician, doctor (especially vet), farmer, astronaut, MI6 operative.

Class Four

Working to live. Your job delivers the cash you need to live comfortably and do what you want to do in your spare time, e.g. advertising executive, window-cleaner, arms salesman, plumber, singing telegram.

---

[1] Yes, *that* Violet Teithe! Former bass guitarist with the Correctettes (later the Tipp-Ex Twins).

[2] *Fluid: An Ideology*. Garlic Press, 1973. 4pp.

According to Teithe, there is something to be said for taking even a Class Four job, provided you *never* pretend to be fulfilled by it.[1]

─────────Getting That Job─────────

There are three ways of getting the job you want. The first and easiest is nepotism. Although the word is derived from the seventeenth-century Italian *nepote* meaning 'nephew', it actually works better for 'nieces', especially pretty ones.

Second, you may be head-hunted. This will only happen if you already have a job in which you seem to be successful.

The third is to fill in a form and go for an interview. The sprezz approach to form-filling is simply stated: if the truth cannot be made to seem sufficiently impressive, you might as well lie.[2]

─────────The Job Interview─────────

The ten questions most often asked at job interviews are the following:

Why do you want this job?
Do you understand the work you'll be doing?
Do you have relevant experience or interests?
Why did you leave your previous employment?
Do you work well as part of a team?

---

[1] For my own refutation of this point, see *Proceedings of the Eighth International Conference Held Entirely For The Sake Of Holding An International Conference* ('ICHEFSOHIC '84'), available in translation from the Sturgis University Press, Kentucky (3 vols).

[2] A recent survey of 177 successful job applicants who had falsely claimed to hold such qualifications as exam passes and degrees, revealed that only 39 (22%) were subsequently asked to produce the relevant bits of paper. Of these, 12 said they had lost them, five produced indifferent forgeries (in three cases these were accepted) and 22 ignored the request. Of the original 177, only nine were sacked and 167 kept their jobs (one committed suicide). If they had all told the truth, none of them would have got their jobs in the first place.

Can you handle responsibility?
How much money do you want?
Is there a danger you'll find the work dull?
What's your ultimate ambition?
Is there anything *you'd* like to ask?
And here are the correct answers:

Why do you want this job?

Well in a sense it was chosen for me. I was thinking of changing the direction of my career, so I wrote a computer programme covering my experience, interests and personal qualities, then I fed in the requirements for 150 different jobs. This particular vacancy gave a 97.24 per cent match, which was ten points clear of the second choice.

Also, I think it might be fun.

Do you understand the work you'll be doing?

Good heavens, I hope not. When you stop learning, in any job, I think it's time to move on. Let me just say that I have a rather vivid[1] conception of the parameters and leave it at that.

Do you have relevant experience or interests?

Relevant in the lateral sense, certainly. I mean, who would have thought that a passion for surrealist art would help to sell cigarettes? But lo and behold – the Benson and Hedges campaign. Right? So in a universe in which everything is relevant to everything else, this particular job is at the geometrical centre of my interests and experiences. There is a sort of confluence. A coming-together. A synthesis.

Why did you leave your previous employment?

Two reasons. One was personal. Can I be frank? Sexual harassment by one of the less attractive directors.[2] The

---

[1] The word 'vivid', used in any context, scores a definite ten.
[2] This line can be used by either sex. *Vive la revolution.* Don't forget the phrase 'less attractive'. As you say it, try to make eye contact and smile at the ugliest member of the opposite sex on the interview panel.

other was the feeling that the rewards – the salary increases, the perks, the praises – were all coming too easily. I wasn't stretching hard enough for them. As Browning said: 'Ah, but a man's reach should exceed his grasp, or what's a heaven for?' I want to be *held down* for a while. Build up a head of steam? You see what I'm getting at?

Do you work well as part of a team?

I think to work well with a team you have to be temperamentally a loner, but with a strong need to interrelate. Independent but connective. Neither subversive nor submersive. The key word is feedback. I've always been a responsive person, but a winger rather than a striker. A goal-*maker*, not a goal-*scorer*.

Can you handle responsibility?

Yes.[1]

Erm, could you expand on that?

Responsibility is never given. It is taken. I am ready to take complete responsibility, from day one, for my own work and that of my subordinates. No passing the buck. No whining. No excuses. No regrets. No apologies.[2] I'm sorry, it's something about which I feel rather strongly.

How much money do you want?

To live the life I want to live at the moment, I need exactly £x[3] a year. Any more would simply go into a deposit account. I wouldn't need it. So that's how much I want. I could survive on a good deal less, of course. If you like I'll make you an offer. Either pay me the going rate, or pay me what you eventually decide I'm worth. I'm prepared to gamble that the latter will be rather more.

Is there a danger you'll find the job dull?

Dull?[4] If anyone says this job is dull, they're not doing it

---

[1] Said without smiling. Use this squelcher once (and once only) during the interview.
[2] Seem to be rather angry here.
[3] A figure exactly 10 per cent higher than the advertised salary.
[4] Laugh as convincingly as possible.

right. 'To see eternity in a grain of sand . . .' I'll go along with Blake. It's a job for someone with a controlled imagination. The control is as important as the imagination. That doesn't make it dull.

What's your ultimate ambition?

I could quote Oliver Herford: 'I've always wanted to throw an egg into an electric fan.'

What you're really asking is[4] how do I define happiness? I think happiness is the click you get when a piece of the jigsaw fits. I just want lots and lots of clicks.

Is there anything you'd like to ask?

Yes. Is there any rule against coming in to work at four in the morning? I find four to seven is one of my most productive times of day.

---

[1] Again, use this form of words once and once only.

Percy Limboule likes to greet a visitor to his office by handing him a blank sheet of paper and saying, 'Here — use this.' Then he busies himself about the room, leaving the visitor holding the paper and feeling foolish.

The Office Environment

A good deal of pointless debate has taken place over the years between the advocates of maximum clutter and the proponents of the sterile cell. Either sort of workplace, taken to its extreme, can be resoundingly sprezzy.

Limboule's office, for example, currently contains several hundred old newspapers and magazines, including incomplete sets of *Oz*, *Private Eye*, *The Times Literary Supplement*, *School Friend* and *Screen International*, a table on which books, chosen for their weight and dustiness and interleaved with paper markers, are stacked six-deep, a great many maps, charts, calendars, files, cardboard boxes, gramophone records, spools of recording tape, telephone directories, tins, lamps, rubber-bands, giant fircones, bulging paper bags, used batteries, sheets of carbon paper and ballpoint pens, and a noticeboard on which now, meaningless lists and reminders are pinned in geological strata.

On the other hand, Wilmot, ever the ascetic, works in a converted wine-cellar which has white walls and a bare concrete floor. His office furniture consists of an armchair. If he needs to make a note of anything he borrows your pen, rolls up his trouser-leg and writes it, in immaculate Pitman's shorthand, on his curiously hairless calf.

Whichever basic environmental style you choose, it is a good idea to have on your office desk a framed photograph. Choose one of the following:

— A vintage Bentley standing on a gravel drive.
— A large Mediterranean villa.
— A rear view of someone in a kagoul manning the helm of a racing yacht in a heavy sea.
— Any war-is-hell combat photograph, provided it is an original print and not taken from a newspaper or magazine.

Practise letting your gaze drift to the photograph and your eyes slowly mist with bittersweet memories.

Do this twice daily until someone asks about the picture. Then, with a tightening of the lips, thrust the frame into a drawer and leave it there.

Before I move on, I must record Limboule's memo ploy. It is his practice, whenever he receives a memo from his boss, to mark it on the bottom with two (not one, never three) exclamation marks and pin it on the wall. Nobody, least of all his boss, has ever asked him what he finds so extraordinary about these memos, but he is treated at work with great respect and circumspection.

———————Telephone Technique———————

It was the great Alastair Glass who first dialled a colleague's extension and said 'Yes?'

Let us pause in reverence for a moment. What single word could be more surrealistically *just so*?

On that first glorious occasion, the Glass yes-ploy unfolded as follows:

Colleague	Uh?
Glass	What is it?
Colleague	What's what? You rang me. Can I help you?
Glass	Problem solved then?
Colleague	What problem?
Glass	Quite. (CLICK)

It is true that Glass became so fond of this wheeze that he overused it dreadfully. He even programmed his telephone answering machine to say 'Yes?'[1]

The ploy became a bit of a joke, and eventually giggling office juniors would wait for Glass's call and answer it with: 'Good morning. Could I speak to "No" please?'

Here are a few more tried and tested phone-ploys:
— Before dialling any UK number, keep your finger on the cut-off button and dial 0101. It looks to anyone watching as though you are ringing the United States. If it is afternoon when you make the call, you should start the conversation with 'Good morning.'

— Keep your telephone in a locked desk drawer. On your day off, ring it frequently.

---

[1] Incidentally, the favoured answering machine message in sprezz circles is currently, 'This is a recorded message. You've got a wrong number.'

— In pub or restaurant, take out a pocket calculator and punch the buttons at random. Hold it to your ear and say, 'Huh, still engaged!'

— In the middle of a call say, 'Would you like to switch to the scrambler at this point? Oh, haven't you got one? Perhaps we'd better not name names then.'

— When told by a snotty secretary that the person you want is unavailable, say, 'In that case I'd like to leave a message. Have you got a pen? OK, here it is: 7486P M28K4 ZYD62 030JQ SC4GU. Will you mark it "urgent" please, and see that I get a reply?'

When the person rings back, say, 'Did you get the message? What? Well, I've heard of people getting things garbled, but this is ridiculous!'

——— TEST PAPER ———

Section A

1. You are attending a formal meeting and a colleague on the same salary as yourself, but with greater experience, asks you to take your feet off the table. Do you:

a. Explain that, because of a strained ligament you sustained playing squash with a client last night, it's the only position in which you are comfortable?

b. Say, 'Piss off George, I'll sit how I like.'?

c. Leap up, polish the table with your handkerchief, and spend the rest of the meeting pacing to and fro like a caged tiger?

2. Your boss's daughter is 21 on Saturday, but nobody from the office has been invited to her party. Do you:

a. Forge an invitation to yourself, using copperplate Letraset, and leave it lying on your desk?

b. Buy her an expensive present in the hope that you will now be added to the guest-list?

c. Persuade your colleagues to gate-crash the party, then spend the evening watching telly?

3. You left school at 16. If asked by a prospective employer why this was, do you reply:

a. 'I felt I'd had enough of academic education. I wanted to start making an impact on the world.'?

b. 'I was already working on my first book.
   Exams would simply have got in the
   way.'?

c. 'They expelled me for selling the cricket
   pavilion to an American tourist.'?

4. A client asks why the work you promised
   to finish for last Monday cannot now be
   completed until the middle of next month.
   Do you say:

a. 'We've had to redesign the CSAs to fit the
   cap-valve capillary distribution system on
   the Type Six. It was either that or junk the
   whole batch and start again.'?

b. 'You're pushing too hard. It's not my own
   stress that bothers me – I'm paid to handle
   it – but some of my people are close to
   cracking up.'?

c. 'As Katherine Graham once remarked, "I
   always thought that if you worked hard
   enough and tried hard enough things
   would work out. I was wrong."'?

5. Which of the following is the most
   suitable Christmas present for a detested
   colleague?

a. A gold electro-plated champagne bottle
   recorker.

b. A pokerwork motto reading 'You Don't
   Have To Be Mad To Work Here But It
   Helps'.

c. An LP of the London Philharmonic
   playing stirring themes from the TV
   commercials.

Section B (Open-ended questions)

1. You are employed by a jobbing builder to type and file invoices. Outline a plan for furthering your career. (You may not organise a price-fixing ring for council contracts, but other proposed illegalities will be judged on merit.)

2. Write down the most original excuse you can think of for taking a day off work. Plausibility will be taken into consideration.

3. Devise a fictional curriculum vitae to accompany an application for one of the following positions:
   — Editor of *Good Housekeeping*.
   — Air Traffic Controller.
   — Estate manager, Sandringham.
   — KGB agent.

Now check your score

Section A

1. A combination of *a* and *c* works well, but *b* is sprezzier. (Score five.)
2. *a* and *b* are pathetic. *c* scores three.
3. Only *c* avoids the defensive note that is fatal at job interviews. Score five unless the prospective employer is American. If the prospective employer is American, score ten.
4. Use all three lines, but stick to this sequence. (Score whatever you like.)
5. Depends who it is, really, doesn't it? (But score five for a decisive answer.)

Answers to open-ended questions are by their nature uncheckable. Don't be so anal.

43

3

GAME, SPREZZ AND MATCH

*Consistency is the last refuge
of the unimaginative.*
Oscar Wilde

In the playing of any game there are two possible sprezz approaches. The first is to take it very seriously indeed. This is particularly effective with games that most people regard as harmless fun, such as bar skittles, charades, frog-racing or Happy Families.

The other approach is to treat the whole thing as a laugh. This approach is advised for games which people take very seriously: chess, golf, bridge, poker, back-gammon and Russian roulette.

How does this work in practice? Let us take the example of wargaming, a hobby which Graham Weaving takes extremely seriously and in which Jimmy Milkwash, because he knows nothing about it, has inevitably to adopt sprezz approach B. The following is a transcript of edited highlights from a game played in January 1985. Scores are given in brackets after each round.

Milkwash	What a fabulous collection of toy soldiers!
Weaving	We prefer to call them military miniatures. So you've not done any wargaming before?
Milkwash	Oh I've fooled around. The other day I was trying out an alternative Waterloo in the pub at lunchtime. I used beermats for the infantry, potato crisps for the cavalry and peanuts for

the artillery. Napoleon still lost I'm
afraid.

Weaving   He shouldn't have, you know.

Milkwash   Well he would have won, but his
cavalry went soggy.[1]
(Milkwash 7, Weaving 4)

Weaving   I thought we might have a go at one
of the more interesting action
sequences from the Boer War.

Milkwash   That's a bit of a euphemism isn't it?
'Action sequence'? You're talking
about battles, massacres, rape,
pillage and murder.

Weaving   We try to leave rape out of it,
actually. It's difficult to simulate in
miniature.

Milkwash   I must say I feel a certain uneasiness
about the idea of turning war into a
game. I mean, every time you knock
over one of those little plastic
soldiers, you're symbolically taking a
human life.

Weaving   Five human lives actually. Each
model represents five men.[2]
(Milkwash 3, Weaving 7)

Weaving   Perhaps I'd better explain the basic
equipment: numbered buttons,
cottonwool balls, cardboard squares,
triangles, discs in various colours,
protractors, rulers, dividers,
compasses, coloured pennants on
cocktail sticks, notepads, pencils (red,
blue and green), cotton, fusewire,

---

[1] Milkwash's 'irreverent dabbler' approach is quite correct.
Never admit total ignorance of a game. The implication
should be that you've done enough in the past to be pretty
sure that you could have been brilliant at it if you hadn't
decided it was a waste of time.

[2] This shows the deadly, if crude, effect of the pedantic plonk.

clocks, egg-timers, mirrors on sticks, tweezers, dice, playing cards, coloured tape, slate and chalks, map-measuring device, pocket calculator, buzzer, rule-books, toy telescope . . .

Milkwash Fine. Shall we start?

Weaving You understand how to use all this?

Milkwash I'm a bit vague about the cottonwool.

Weaving Smoke. You get a lot of smoke on a battlefield. Reduced visibility. We simulate it with cottonwool.

Milkwash Fine. I thought it might be to put in our ears so we won't be deafened by the artillery. Shall we start?

Weaving In a moment. Now, you see this bundle of file-cards? This one tells you how much fodder is required by your cavalry, according to the terrain, rainfall and distance covered. That's very important. If you run out of fodder you have to start shooting your horses.

This one tells you how accurate your artillery can be at different ranges. You've got grapeshot, shrapnel and high-explosive in various calibres with crosswind and visibility in the left-hand column. Same again for your small arms, and on this one you've got water and field-rations. Now these green cards give you your degrees of casualty. A green card with a red cross on it is for the walking wounded, a blue cross for the stretcher cases and a black cross for fatalities.

Milkwash Corpses.[1]

---

[1] Milkwash is here driven back to basic strategy. He keeps the irritation factor going while waiting for an opening.

Weaving	Quite. Now these yellow cards cover morale – low, high and average, with the variable factors affecting morale set out along the top. For instance, if you get a letter from home, your morale goes up.
Milkwash	Wouldn't that depend on what's in the letter?
Weaving	It says here 'Morale goes up'. All right? Let's not make this thing any more complicated than it needs to be.
Milkwash	God forbid.[1]

(Milkwash 6, Weaving 9)

Predictably, two hours into the game, Milkwash was losing badly. Playing the part of General Methuen at the battle of Magersfontein, he was being cut to ribbons by his Boer opponent. However, at this point he staged a late recovery:

Weaving	Come on. You haven't moved any men for fifteen minutes.
Milkwash	Ah. New developments, y'see. I've worked out where I'm going wrong. It's my motivation. I need to care passionately about winning. At the moment it's just a game.
Weaving	Just do your best.
Milkwash	Ah well, I've got the solution. My crack divisions have decided to become Communists.
Weaving	They can't. They didn't have Communists in the Boer War. I'm sure they didn't.
Milkwash	Are we going to be mere slaves to history, or can I fight this battle my own way, hm?
Weaving	But you're not fighting.

---

[1] A rather weak rejoinder, but it salvages a couple of points.

Milkwash	They're having a meeting.
Weaving	What about?
Milkwash	Whether to execute their commanding officer and declare support for the principles laid down in Marx's great address to the second congress of the First International of the Communist Party, which I happen to know was translated into English in 1899.
Weaving	Get on with it.
Milkwash	Just a moment. They're taking a vote. The motion is 'that this revolutionary military commune is prepared to fight to the last man'. Oh dear.
Weaving	What?
Milkwash	The motion has been overwhelmingly defeated. They seem to feel that this is a war of capitalist colonial exploitation, and they want nothing more to do with it. Sorry.
	(Milkwash 10, Weaving nil)

Milkwash wins 26–20.

——————Creative Rule-Changing——————

A player can engineer a better chance of winning at board games and cards by suggesting an apparently innocuous change to the rules. For example, in Monopoly you might proceed as follows:

'You know, the best games of Monopoly I ever had were with a bunch of law students at Oxford. We played according to the real laws of property speculation: planning permission, listed buildings, short-term leases, variable interest rates, all the rest of it. I don't suggest we do the same – we haven't got the time or the reference books to hand – but there was one change to the official rules that livened it up no end: introducing the concept of risk-insurance. You could buy and sell insurance to cover the risk of landing on a certain property. The usual

Raymond Lobswill would regularly win at hide and seek by putting up so pathetic a pretence of 'being a tree' that the seeker would not have the heart to 'spot' him.

premium was a tenth of the rent for that property per circuit of the board. Any takers?'

Having introduced the concept, let the others make the running. Let them 'get the hang of it' by sorting out their own little deals, while you play your normal game. Put together a couple of sets, build a few houses. (A word of advice: go for pink and brown, and put three houses on each property. Don't touch the railway stations or the utilities.) Then, when cash-flow problems start to bite all round, offer your insurance policies at cut-rate (say 7 per cent of rental) to cover no more than 45 per cent of your medium-risk properties, with a no-refund clause in the event of houses being sold and properties mortgaged during the term of the policy.

Do not buy any insurance yourself. If asked why you don't, say, 'I like to live dangerously.' Then, if you lose, you will go down in a blaze of buccaneering glory. If you win, the victory will be twice as sweet.

Here are some 'creative amendments' to the rules of other games:

Poker

Players who have 'folded' their own cards are free to contract side-bets between themselves on the eventual winner of the hand. This makes it possible for an indifferent player to win at poker simply by recognising talent in others.

Bridge

Remove the two, three, four and five of each suit, and deal nine cards to each player. Everyone else will find themselves overbidding their hands until they get used to the new game. Meanwhile, you should have built up a commanding lead.

Pontoon

Just as an ace can be counted as 'one' or 'eleven', so, under your proposed amendment, a two can be twelve, a three can be thirteen and so on. Other players, until they adapt, will tend to stick too low.

Scrabble

For 'double' and 'triple' read 'half' and 'third'. The aim of the game becomes to *avoid* the coloured squares. This amendment ruins the game for the Scrabble strategist and benefits the tactical or 'seat of the pants' player. If you are good at Scrabble in the first place, don't suggest it. If you're a comparatively mediocre player, the rule will bother your opponent far more than it bothers you.

Cluedo

The player who wants to advance a hypothesis ('Professor Plum in the Ballroom with the Lead Piping') has to collect the murder weapon in question from its previous location and *take* it to the part of the board where the accusation is to be made. This makes for a lot more dashing around the board, slows the game up considerably and makes it rather more a matter of chance and correspondingly less a matter of deductive ability. It is therefore a helpful amendment for the stupid player.

Draughts

Pieces which have made it to the other side of the board ('crowns') and then all the way back again, become 'double crowns' and cannot be captured at all. The winner becomes the player who, when all the other pieces have been taken, is left with the greater number of 'double crowns'. Again, this change undermines strategy and benefits tactical play.

Tiddlywinks

All squoops are inverted.[1]

Chess

Chess is so thoroughly a game of sprezzatura that some aficionados have gone so far as to spell it 'chezz'.[2]

There is a vast literature available to anyone who wants to become a better player, and it is worth a glance, if only

---

[1] This rule benefits nobody, but you derive a psychological advantage from suggesting it, especially when playing against young children.

[2] Lorna Sprinkle tried to popularise the word 'spress' but it never caught on.

because it teaches you words like 'zugzwang'.[1]

The following brief suggestions hint at an approach which may suit the player who is concerned to succeed at chess without being terribly good at it.[2]

On the board in your living room, set out a textbook endgame. Invite your opponent to play it out with you. If you win, that's fine. If your opponent wins in six moves say: 'Hm. It was supposed to be mate in four.'

Allow your opponent to set out the pieces for the first game, then, while he or she rummages under the table for a pawn you have 'accidentally' knocked on the floor, deftly reverse the positions of the white king and queen. As your opponent returns to contemplating the board, reach across and correct them with a superior smile.

Take an early opportunity to remark:

'At a certain level it's more satisfying to play a doomed romantic attacking game and fall apart in a shower of brilliant sparks, than to plod through to stalemate on pure positional play, don't you think?'

If your opponent doesn't blunder after a remark like this, at least you've covered yourself for losing.

Bernard Gorridge wins regularly against superior opponents by the simple device of saying, at a crucial point in the game, 'Go on. Astonish me.'

It was Gorridge who also perfected the Blindman's Opening. He will habitually make his first three moves verbally ('Pawn to king's third', etc.) while staring out of the window. This unsettles his opponent in three ways:

First, by making him wonder whether it is Bernard's intention to play the whole game without looking at the board. Could it be that the man is blind and hasn't mentioned the fact? *Why* doesn't he look at the board? Such speculation is very damaging to the concentration.

Second, by demonstrating supreme confidence that, whatever the opponent's moves, Bernard will be able to

---

[1] 'A situation in which it is impossible to move without making matters worse.' 'Zugzwang' was accorded first place, two years running, in the annual Sprezzatura Enterprises survey, 'Your Hundred Most Useful Words'.

[2] See also Sprinkle's classic, *Chess is Like a Glass of Lemon Tea*. Behemoth Press, 1977.

cope. (In fact his three opening moves are always the same anyway.)

Third, by making the opponent worry whether he should announce his own opening moves in the same way.

The secret of a successful Blindman's Opening is to let the silence build. After Bernard's 'pawn to king's third' he continues to stare out of the window. His opponent makes his own move. Bernard takes no notice. The opponent clears his throat nervously. Nothing. The opponent now says, 'Your move', or even 'Erm, pawn to king's third likewise ha ha, erm.'

Bernard then says very quickly: 'Knight to QB three.'

Weak opponents have been known to resign after three moves.

Sport

Sports may be divided into four categories, as follows:

Group A Those which have sprezz-potential for participants, but not for spectators, e.g. squash, sailing, climbing, hang-gliding, crazy golf.
Group B Those which it may be sprezzy to watch, but no one should actually join in, e.g. football, horse-racing, lacrosse, basketball, kite-flying.
Group C Those which can be sprezzy both to do and to watch, e.g. tennis, cricket, billiards, polo, rowing.
Group D Those which have no sprezz-potential whatever, e.g. potholing, snooker, darts, ten-pin bowling, figure-skating.

The thing to remember about participation sports (Groups A and C) is that you don't have to be better than your opponent, you only have to be better than expected (considering how much less seriously you take the game).

You are, or at any rate aim to be, a gifted amateur. The less gifted you are, the more amateur you must seem. Do not turn up on the golf course in check trousers and a Lee Trevino sweater, carrying a bag of custom-made clubs. Arrive in jeans and a duffle-coat ('Bit nippy this morning. I hope we're not going to dawdle. Just bang 'em in and sod the finer points . . .'), ask to share your opponent's 'sticks' and say: 'Have I got this right? It's the one with the *lowest* score who wins?' Then put into practice everything you have learned in your secret sessions with the club pro.

If you are very bad indeed at your chosen sport, you will need to come up with a reason for being quite as awful as you are. The Norman Neumann ambidextrous gambit is recommended for failures at squash, golf, shooting, tennis and cricket. After a particularly humiliating thrashing, take an early opportunity to switch your watch to the opposite wrist, write something down with your pen in the wrong hand, and eat your lunch with your knife and fork reversed. If your opponent comments on this:

'I didn't know you were left (right)-handed,' (or even if not), you reply:

'I'm trying to make myself ambidextrous by using the wrong hand all the time, but it's a bit of a struggle.'

The beauty of Neumann's gambit is that your opponent won't know whether you're referring to the match you've just so spectacularly lost, or to your eating habits.

Three other gambits deserve mention in the context of participation sports. The first is:

'Mine is a different and superior game'

Scene: a squash court. Baldock versus Spume. Baldock has just scored five points in a row.

Spume	(panting heavily) Revoy!
Baldock	Eh?
Spume	Sorry, I was forgetting. This is squash, isn't it?
Baldock	What did you think it was?
Spume	It's so similar to pelota in some respects. I keep wanting to *catch* the ball. It makes it very awkward. And you see, every time you cross in front of me, I instinctively want to shout 'Revoy!' I really must concentrate. I have to remind myself this is only a weedy little rubber ball. If it hits me, IT IS NOT GOING TO KILL ME. But one gets so used to not taking chances . . .

(etc. All of which is complete garbage, of course. Spume

Drawn to play against B. J. Lorrimer in the quarter finals of the golf club's annual knock-out tournament, Leonard 'Pinko' Smithers introduces himself.

Purely to unsettle his opponent, he wears a jacket with an unusually long right sleeve and shakes hands, awkwardly, with the left.

has never played pelota in his life. All he knows about it is that it's something Spaniards play very fast with wicker-work scoops. 'Revoy' is a made-up word. Nevertheless, Baldock must now feel that his victory is somehow hollow.)

Variations of the same ploy can be used in many other sports, e.g. football (or rugby):

'Once a year I get to play real football. Well, I say "football", it's actually "fotebal". The mediaeval version. They play it at Ashbourne on Shrove Tuesday. The playing area is ten miles of open country — rivers, barbed-wire fences, brambles, the lot. They have about 200 players on each team. The game goes on for six hours, and you're allowed to do anything except use knives. It makes conventional soccer look a bit tame, a bit *hidebound* . . .'

Or, to take another example, martial arts:

'What you have to remember is that these techniques were originally designed to disable or kill your opponent. There's no point in learning the moves if you don't learn to do them properly, and then, of course, it becomes much too dangerous. My instructor was lucky; he learned his stuff during the war, when that sort of thing didn't matter so much, and any little accidents could be written off. But if you came at me now, I'd automatically bring my hand up like that and burst your eardrum. I couldn't help myself. It's a conditioned reflex . . .' (etc. etc.)

Or fishing:

'I realise there's an art to fishing for everything from perch to hammerhead sharks, but I'm afraid once you've had a fighting barracuda on the line, you're rather spoiled for trout and salmon . . .'

Or shooting:

'If you've ever seen a man's face in the cross-hairs, and squeezed the trigger, I think it's hard to take shooting at cardboard very seriously. It's almost blasphemous in a way . . .'[1]

'Let me help you'

Scene: a cricket field. Roote is batting. Limboule is

---

[1] Further questioning to be answered: 'It's something I don't really talk about . . .'

keeping wicket (very badly). Roote slices at a googly which arcs back over his head. Limboule misses the easiest catch of the game. He picks up the ball, studies it thoughtfully and addresses the goggling Roote:

Limboule   Really, Simon. You shouldn't have had any problems there. Can I give you a word of advice? You're not tracking the ball. It's a matter of watching its parabola and then extending it, mentally, to the point where it meets the bat, rather than just swinging at it hopefully. And don't be afraid to clout the thing. OK? (He tosses the ball back to the bowler, and calls to him.) Oi, David! Give us another googly. Simon wants to try that stroke again . . .

And finally, there's:

'If you knew as much about this lark as I do . . .'

Scene: a rock face in North Wales. Selina Quark is about to abseil down a fifty-foot cliff when know-all Jeremy Neck approaches:

Jeremy   You've got your rope threaded wrong, Selina. It should go *round* there and *through* the metal bit.

Selina   Wasn't that how Stan Churton killed himself? (Jeremy blushes beneath his beard and traverses quickly away.)

Myself   Stan Churton?

Selina   It was the first name that sprang to mind.

Groups B and C: Spectator Sports

There is only one basic sprezz-ploy here. In the words of the poet Keats it is 'all ye know on earth and all ye need to know'. It is simply to see things others miss, and if you can't see things others miss, imagine them. Half a dozen examples should suffice.

Rugby

'He's a useful fly-half, but he always tends to veer to the left. Too predictable . . .' (Fly-half gets trodden on) 'See what I mean?'

Cricket

'Oh-oh. It looks as though Kellaway's knee-cartilage is playing up again. He positively hobbled on that last delivery.'

Billiards

'If he'd gone for the in-off instead of the cannon, he could have lined himself up on the top pocket. Ah well . . .'

Tennis

'She's putting too much back-spin on her lobs. That's why they're all over the place.'

Football

'Do you realise that out of the thirty-six times he's played the ball so far, Logburst hasn't once hit it on the volley?'

Horse-racing

'Penthouse Pet looks good on paper but her nostrils are set too close together. Probably why she sweats so much.'[1]

---

[1] This line can also be used for Martina Navratilova.

There is only one thing less sprezzy than winning second place in a knobbly knees competition, and that is being a bad loser.

TEST PAPER

Section A

1. You are invited to play bezique, a card game of which you are entirely ignorant. Do you reply:

a. 'It's a while since I've played. Perhaps I could look over your shoulder for a couple of hands, just to refresh my memory?' (Then tut and shake your head a great deal)?

b. 'Not me. Last time I played bezique I dropped 400 quid.'?

c. 'Sure. I play the New Orleans version. It's bezique with a touch of Montana red dog. Shall we say a pound a point, and I'll explain the rules as we go along'?

2. Your 8-year-old niece challenges you to a round of crazy golf. At the eleventh hole she is seventeen strokes ahead. Do you:

a. Whack your ball into the boating lake and suggest you call it a draw?

b. Surreptitiously jam half a brick inside the helter-skelter hazard at the fifteenth hole, and wait patiently as she struggles in vain to negotiate the blocked orifice?

c. Play on to a resounding defeat and then send her for an ice-cream while you remark to her parents: 'At that age it does no harm to let them win occasionally'?

3. You have been fishing for hours without success. How do you respond to the cheery greeting, 'Caught anything yet?'?

a. 'I had one who fought me for the best part of twenty minutes. When I got him ashore I said, "You deserve to live, matey," and chucked him back.'

b. 'I had one enormous bugger on the line, but he bent the hook straight' (displaying hook carefully straightened with needle-nosed pliers and kept in pocket for this purpose).

c. 'The water temperature's 4.2 and the caddis fly are hatching in the big pool. There's nitrate fertiliser on the farmland over there and the river's down 6 inches at Barnaby Reach. Caught anything? You've got to be joking!'

4. You have invested a fiver in the pub's fruit machine without a significant win. Asked how you're getting on, you reply:

a. 'I've got the sequences on the first three reels. Once I've got the fourth reel worked out and memorised, I'll be ready to start winning.'

b. The statistical probability of a jackpot on the next twenty goes is one in eleven. When I started it was one in forty-two. I'm making steady progress.'

c. 'The profits from this machine go to the old folks' Christmas party, so I'm not bothered about blowing a fiver on it occasionally.'

5. Although terrified of heights (you like to open your umbrella before stepping off the bus), you are invited to go up in a hot-air balloon. Do you reply:

a. 'Without oxygen equipment we're not going to get much beyond 30,000 feet. It hardly seems worth it.'?

b. 'I'd love to, but I must warn you, I always get very silly in balloons. Last time Jeremy was convinced I was going to throw him over the side. I let him back in the basket eventually, of course . . .'?

c. 'I'm only coming if we can take Auntie Nellie. I'm sure if anything's going to cure her airsickness, this will.'?

Section B (Open-ended questions)

1. Charades. Describe in detail (with diagrams) how you would act:

a. *A Contribution to the Critique of Political Economy* by Karl Marx.

b. *Ubu Roi.*

c. *The Hunchback of Notre Dame.* (Points will be awarded for dignity.)

2. Using a tennis ball, up to three pieces of driftwood and a plastic bucket, invent a beach game that you can be fairly sure you will win.

3. There's a breathless hush in the close tonight –
Ten to make and the match to win –
A bumping pitch and a blinding light,
An hour to play and the last man in.
And it's not for the sake of a ribboned coat,

Or the selfish hope of a season's fame,
But his captain's hand on his shoulder smote –
'Play up! Play up! and play the game.'
Vitaï Lampada by Henry Newbolt.

a. What, in those circumstances, would *you* have said to the batsman?

b. In a situation in which the sand of the desert was sodden red, the Gatling jammed and the Colonel dead, would your advice be any different? If so, how?

Now check your score

1. *a* and *b* are OK for novices. Score two. *c* is only for advanced sprezzpersons. Score nil or ten accordingly.
2. *b* is the preferred answer ('Show me a good loser and I'll show you a loser' – Henry Cooper). But shouldn't you have done it sooner? Score three.
3. *a* scores nil. (Did you spot the trap? The use of the word 'matey' is unforgivable). *b* scores three. *c* scores five as long as there is no possibility of the counter, 'There's a bloke further down who's caught half a dozen.'
4. *a* and *b* are obsessional. *c* hits the correct tone of insouciance. Score five.
5. It's not what you say, it's the way that you say it. Could you make these lines work? Be honest. You could? Fair enough, score five.

4
MATTERS OF TASTE

*One man's meat is another
man's posing.*
Toby Fruin

*The golden rule is that there
are no golden rules.*
George Bernard Shaw

Taste, they will tell you, is a personal thing. Everybody's different, they insist. Just because you like to keep your beermat collection in a funfur Gremlin pyjama-case, just because you wear a BBC Breakfast Time teeshirt, just because you like David Essex and your favourite poet is Erica Jong, just because you send birthday cards with airbrush pictures of semi-nude men in white socks on the front, and just because your cruet set is disguised as Tower Bridge, others have no right to criticise, sneer or mutter the word 'naff'.

It may surprise you to learn that this is essentially the sprezz point of view on matters of taste. The classic formulation is Cooney's: **'Sprezz is the enemy of good taste.'**[1]

What, after all, is 'good taste'? It is the fashionable consensus among those who consider themselves to be socially and intellectually superior. In sprezz terms, it is the facade of certainty which you are in business to undermine and humiliate.

There are three ways of doing this.[2]

---

[1] Petunia Cooney, *Karl Denver Rules: A Grab-bag of Alternative Obsessions. Wimoweh Press, 1984.*

[2] A motion to amend this to four by the admission of the

Approach no. 1: 'My taste is better than yours'

Those who subscribe to absolute canons of taste, who like what it seems they *ought* to like, are vulnerable to the suggestion that there is a higher and subtler good taste which they do not share.

Here is Molly Casperson letting the air out of Barney Hilpe:

Hilpe   I don't suppose a truly great work of cinema has emerged since *Les Enfants du Paradis*.

Casperson   And yet, even then, cinema was already being corrupted by the notion that film is about dramatic lighting.

Hilpe   Superb lighting in that film . . .

Casperson   Hence the fondness for chiaroscuro as a substitute for any more profound analysis of the nature of light. You could watch *Enfants* and never know that Monet had existed.

Hilpe   So what's *your* favourite film?

Casperson   As a work of total cinema? I think probably *Bambi*.

Approach no. 2: Pack up your troubles in your old kitsch bag

Your own taste cannot be criticised because you make a point of enjoying that which is conventionally regarded as vulgar. Even better, you delight in the captivating hideousness of that which others thought was actually rather nice.

Toby Fruin, glancing over Lemuel Pugh's bookcase: Ah, Skivertex!

Pugh   Sorry?

Penkridge Universal Wince was defeated by over 20,000 votes on a show of cards at the 1983 Annual Delegate Conference of the Sprezzatura Association of Great Britain.

Fruin   Your set of Dickens. I love those simulated leather book club editions with the imitation gold lettering and the sleazy little bookmarks.

Pugh   I happen to like Dickens and I thought that edition was rather good value.

Fruin   Absolutely. The introductions are hilarious. Rubbish, of course, but terribly amusing.

Pugh   I suppose you've got a set of first editions?

Fruin   Good heavens no. I buy Penguin Classics and simply replace them when they wear out.

Approach no. 3: Parton's Pleasure

This, perhaps the most potent approach of all, is named after Dolly Parton, who once remarked: 'I could be very stylish if I chose to be, but I would never stoop so low as to be fashionable.'[1]

The suggestion is that your taste is timeless, indeed classic, whereas that of your sprezzvictim is merely the froth and bubble on some passing wave of popular enthusiasm.

Vanessa Bleache   Have I shown you our bathroom since we had it modernised? Sunken bath, deep-pile cream carpet, step-in shower, bidet, rubber-plants . . .

Penelope Fohne   I noticed it when I washed my hands. I must say I was particularly struck by the quietness of your plumbing. It positively trickles. Ours rumbles and gushes rather. But then, we have one of those impossible Victorian bathrooms that you either love or hate. A huge bathtub with claw feet and taps that could power a hydro-

---

[1] Unkind critics have suggested that Miss Parton would find it difficult in any circumstances to stoop without falling over.

electric turbine. But that's my kind of bathroom – a great, steamy cavern full of rubber ducks and loofahs and barbells and washing-lines, where you can feel cold tiles under your feet and smell Wright's Coal Tar Soap; where you can come home from a long walk, park your muddy wellies in the corner and jump straight in for a good old wallow; a bathroom where you can wash a couple of labradors without making a mess. I'm just not a gold-plated dolphin sort of person, I suppose.

Bleache   The bidet's terribly useful.

Fohne   I'm sure it is. God knows how the other 99 per cent of us manage.

The suggestions that follow, based on these three approaches (sometimes in combination), are grouped according to subject matter.

Television

Whereas it is clearly untrue to say that television has killed the art of conversation, it is certainly the case that the abolition of television would leave us with precious little to discuss.

The Luddites among us may as well admit that discussion of the box is now the major battlefield in any struggle for conversational supremacy. It is no longer good enough to say, 'I never watch. There always seems to be something more important to do.'[1]

McLuhan said, and I agree with him,[2] 'The medium is the message.' To criticise the content of a television programme is therefore to miss the point. Address

---

[1] 'In any conversation, to score a point in such a way that you are thereby prevented from scoring any further points, is to lose a point.' – Herbage.

[2] A form of words first used by Field Marshal Montgomery, in reference to Our Lord.

yourself instead to its stylistic and technical presentation. These, after all, are the only aspects of programme-making that seriously concern the people in the business.

Here is a selection of suitably plonking remarks:

'If only a director would have the courage to take the camera *in among* the actors, instead of just pointing it at them.'

'It's a shame that plays have to be shot on VT[1] rather than film. It's not so much the oily sheen you get on the exterior shots, it's the loss of subtlety in the editing.'

'The test of a good soap opera is whether you can follow the plot with the sound turned off. The Americans understand this but the British don't.'

'Television is about eye-contact. That's why autocue presentation is always unsatisfactory – it makes the presenter's eyes flicker.'

'No television director understands how to use colour. Which is a pity, because they've all forgotten how to work in black and white.'

'So many programmes are ruined because the sound levels are constant. A whisper should be quieter than a shout.'

'If the transcript of a television programme doesn't tell the story, then it was a bad television programme. Too many producers sacrifice coherence for the sake of the visuals.'

'If the transcript of a television programme tells the story, then it was a bad television programme. If the visuals aren't crucial, it might as well have been published in *The Listener* in the first place.'

Radio

The 'I may be old-fashioned but . . .' approach to radio is now obsolete.[2] No points are awarded for catch-phrases

---

[1] VT is short for videotape, as you know.
[2] As is the use of the word 'wireless', which was chic until quite recently.

from 'ITMA', impressions of the 'Radio Doctor', or familiarity with the early history of 'The Archers'. The death of Janet Tregorran in that awful crash in 1963 no longer stirs the passions it once did.

Today, there are two, and only two, lines to take about radio:

1. Radio is about to be, if it is not already, more important than television. TV, 'chewing gum for the eyes' as Fred Allen called it, is heading steadily and inevitably downmarket in pursuit of ratings, while radio holds the high ground.

Have in your living room a copy of *Radio Times*, open at the radio pages, in which certain of the programmes are underlined in red felt-tip. You need not confine yourself to Radio 3. Several programmes on Radio 4 are worth underlining, even if they're not worth listening to. If you stretch to Radios 1 or 2, underline not programme titles but the names of producers and contributors, suggesting that you must remember to switch on and hear this or that old chum do his or her bit on, as it might be, the John Dunn Show.

2. Walkmanship. A portable radio with a set of light-weight headphones is a crucial prop. Take it with you to restaurants, parties, cricket matches, weddings and business conferences. Choose your moment, glance at your watch, pop on the cans,[1] and turn up the volume. After five minutes of nodding sagely and perhaps jotting down a note or two, switch off the set, say 'Sorry' with bright insincerity, and return your attention to your surroundings.

Charlton Pincus, who developed Walkmanship long before those wonderful Sony people gave it a name (in fact he used to lug round a bakelite Pye valve job with an extension mains cable and a pair of home-made head-phones cobbled together out of two telephone handsets and an egg-poacher) may have carried the ploy to excess, but he never *ever* divulged the crucial information: what was he hearing that produced his faraway smile, his

---

[1] Headphones, for those who have not yet taken the Sprezza-tura Enterprises ten-day induction course in jargonautics.

occasional snort of derision, his even more occasional wince of sheer agony?[1] The nearest he came to it was when Pippa Brewster-Quilp, who was by this time starting to smell a rat, pressed him hard on the subject:

Pippa	But *why* do you have to listen to the radio? What were you listening to?
Charlton	You mean just now? Or why do I listen in general?
Pippa	Just now. You were tapping your foot. What was it?
Charlton	I always tap my foot when I'm concentrating.
Pippa	What were you concentrating *on*?
Charlton	The radio. I was having to concentrate because you were making such a racket.
Pippa	But what were you listening to?
Charlton	Or to be more grammatical, to what was I listening?
Pippa	What *was* it, dammit?
Charlton[2]	Actually, it was just that Charles had a little piece on, and he wanted me to catch it and give him an opinion.
Pippa	Charles who?
Charlton	(LAUGHS) Oh dear, Pippa, you can be very cruel when you choose to be . . .

Films

Again, the approach should be obsessively technical.
Question: why is *Jules et Jim* a great film?
Answer: because it includes a scene in which the camera dollies through 360 degrees.

---

[1] The only exception to the Pincus rule is Bastable's 'seafarer' gambit. Tune into the Radio 4 long-wave shipping forecast and *write it down*.

[2] Twenty-six lines have been edited from the text at this point, on grounds of tedium.

Learn the jargon. Talk about 'low-budget action features', 'B-rated oaters' and 'semi-remakes'. Discuss film-stock ('After 1959, 35 mil. Eastmancolor revolutionised studio lighting'), sound balance ('There are those who will tell you that Leone's brilliance lay in photographing sweat, but I think it was his courage in consistently peaking his wild-track at four'), and the intricacies of direction ('There's a superstition that you should never pan and zoom at the same time, but that's what hand-held shooting is all about').

Freddie Bealby makes a point of videotaping extremely bad old movies from Channel 4. Then he insists on replaying 'brilliant' two-minute extracts for his bemused guests. The bits are chosen entirely at random, but Bealby chortles, slaps his thighs, rolls his eyes, bounces in his chair and hugs himself. Then he spools back and plays the scene again. And again. And again.

Guest   I don't see what's so marvellous about it.

Bealby   Ha ha. Tee hee. Watch the guy on the left . . . Did you see? Brilliant! Whoo! Best thing in the film!

Guest   I missed it . . .

Bealby   Watch it again.

At parties, Bealby does a double act with Laura Mackeson in which they act out a dull little scene from *Woman in the Dark* (1934), a forgettable picture starring Melvyn Douglas. It is not their word-perfect delivery that impresses, nor is it their dramatic skills, which are rudimentary; it is the fact that they apparently expect everybody present to identify the reference.

Theatre

When invited to express an opinion about a play, never say, 'I quite liked it,' or 'Not really my cup of tea.' If in doubt, select your critical barbs from the following quiver:

Alan Ayckbourn   – 'Mrs Dale's Diary' as rewritten by Cecil B. De Mille.

American Comedy   – Ramshackle.

Stephen Berkoff — He won't be happy until actors learn to speak through their bottoms.

Alan Bleasdale — Overripe.

Edward Bond — Shows how low you have to sink to repel an audience.

Berthold Brecht — I've heard of alienation but this is ridiculous.

Anton Chekhov — Too much pathos, not enough threat.

T. S. Eliot — Philosophically an antithesis rather than a synthesis.

Farce — Lacks repose.

Feminist drama — Unforgivably masculine.

Trevor Griffiths — The sort of writer who demonstrates solidarity with the workers by licking his plate at the Ritz.

Ronald Harwood — Sags in the middle. Also at both ends.

Henrik Ibsen — Nobody seems to realise he was writing comedy.

Arthur Miller — Presents truisms as truth.

Musical — Pre-pubertal.

John Osborne — Too loud.

Harold Pinter — Writes for the ear, not the eye.

Stephen Poliakoff — All the resonance of a concrete violin.

Dennis Potter — Too easily shocked by himself.
and

	Too much treacle, not enough brimstone.
J. B. Priestley	– Underrated by the actors, overrated by the audience.
Frederic Raphael	– A ventriloquist with a broken doll.
Terence Rattigan	– Gave the well-made play a bad name. and The gloss of mahogany-finish Formica.
Restoration drama	– A timid version.
Willy Russell	– Soap opera.
Peter Schaeffer	– Writes for the eye, not the ear.
W. Shakespeare	– Should be played as though it's noon in the desert. This production made it midnight.[1]
George Bernard Shaw	– Phony paradoxes strung together like onions.
Neil Simon	– Rots the teeth.
Oscar Wilde	– Phony paradoxes strung together like pearls.

It was, incidentally, George Bernard Shaw who remarked: 'You don't expect me to know what to say about a play when I don't know who the author is, do you?'

Art

A frightening number of conceptual artists (two).
Fran Lebowitz

In his old age, Vlaminck was shown a selection of paintings bearing his name and invited to pick out the forgeries. He had no idea which were the genuine

---

[1] Vice versa for the comedies, of course.

Vlamincks and which were the worthless imitations. There is a lesson here. Since only one person in a thousand can tell the difference between a 'good' painting and a 'bad' one, and since everyone else feels deeply insecure about their own taste, it is disgustingly easy to furnish your home with works of art which look as though they must have been expensive.

For example, instead of buying and framing half a dozen poster prints of the better-known works of Van Gogh or Picasso, you can pick up, for the same money, a couple of original paintings by second-year design students at your local polytechnic. *And no one will know they're crap.*

If you prefer to go for prints, choose obscure ones and sign each with the artist's name and a number under 200 before framing it.

Or you might like to try the do-it-yourself approach. Jackson Pollocks are easy to copy but rather old hat. So why not take 50 or 60 square feet of canvas (half the roof of an old tent is ideal), stretch it over chipboard, give it a coat of tangerine emulsion and spray-paint across it in purple the word 'Meshiriya'[1]?

For visits to galleries, the recommended line is: 'Never mind the pretentious bullshit — you either like it or you don't.'

Here is Phil Bixham at the preview of the Royal Academy's Chagall Exhibition:

Anna Molding	Why does he put so many goats in his pictures?
Bixham	(mock-pretentious) For Chagall, the goat represents, I suspect, everyday life. It symbolises the continuity of the mundane.
Molding	In what sense exactly?
Bixham	You know . . . goat to work, goat to lunch, goat to bed . . .
Molding	(warming to him) Oh Phil, you're impossible!

---

[1] A Kikuyu word meaning 'deep creative thoughts'.

There are those who put their faith in quantity, and you can't knock it. A room lined with crowded bookshelves is an impressive prop for anyone who can afford to assemble it. Those of us who can't have to give the impression that our books are in another room – perhaps a study, perhaps an attic – and the measly few we keep in the living room are only the ones we've been glancing at of late. One way to do this is to mention a book, undertake to find a copy ('I know I've got it somewhere'), disappear for fifteen minutes and return, blowing dust off the volume in question, with the line, 'It took a bit of finding. It had got in among the Polynesian section for some reason . . .'

There was a time when a reputation as an intellectual could be acquired simply by carrying a copy of Kierkegaard's *Journals*, title outwards, in one's pocket. Nowadays such crudity is regarded, and rightly, as equivalent to wearing an 'I am an egghead' teeshirt, but Percy Limboule still uses the underlying concept. He takes with him on train journeys a well-thumbed copy of the RAND Corporation's *A Million Random Digits with 100,000 Normal Deviates* and leaves it on the table when he goes to the buffet.

One of the most impressive bits of 'business' involving books was perfected by the Oxford linguistics don, Christopher Tolkien.[1] He would, in the course of a tutorial, make reference to a particular quotation. Then, still talking, his gaze fixed on the undergraduate wallowing in the armchair before him, he would cross to the book-shelves, take down the book, open it – *without looking* – at the correct page, and start to read.

How was it done? Some thought he used a tiny indentation in the spine of the book to guide his hand to the right volume, and lodged a matchstick between the pages to make it open in the right place. Others thought he merely picked a book at random, opened it at random, and then quoted from memory. But the majority view was that he simply devoted several weeks of each

---

[1] Son of J. R. R. 'The Hobbit' Tolkien.

vacation to practising his unique skill.

However, all of this is strictly second-division stuff. If you really want to cut a dash in the world of literature, you need to write books as well as read them. This is not as difficult as it sounds. The hard part is getting the stuff published, but such is the time-lag between submitting a manuscript to a publisher and receiving the rejection that you can safely announce, 'I'm writing a book for X' (naming a well-known publisher), because by the time you get a verdict (if you ever do) everyone will have forgotten about it.

It is, moreover, widely understood that the authors of truly great books, particularly first novels, collect rejection slips the way other people collect parking tickets. Only well-known newscasters and game-show hosts get their stuff into print at the first attempt.

I personally despise Bertha Jitterbug[1] who keeps on her kitchen table a thick volume marked 'Work in Progress' into which she copies fine-sounding chunks of prose from distinguished but little-read authors.[2] True, anyone who sneaks a peep is sure to be impressed, and if the odd quotation *is* recognised, it's not the end of the world ('I treat my commonplace book as an anthology of stylistic models as well as a sort of adventure playground, a place to flex my writing muscles . . .' etc.). But what if she suddenly became a television personality and had to produce 50,000 words at short notice, hm?

Here is a list of books which you could sprezzily claim to be writing:

The Ultra Dame – a biography of Frank Birch, fellow of King's College, Cambridge, leading codebreaker at Bletchley Park during the Second World War and one of the finest Widow Twankeys ever to grace the West End stage.[3]

The Greaseman's Book of US Radio – an anthology of

---

[1] Not his real name.
[2] 'The books that everybody admires are those that nobody reads' – Anatole France.
[3] This is true.

wacky and suggestive transcripts from FM phone-in shows.[1]

Year of the Duck – an account of twelve months spent as a contract assassin for a Chinese crime syndicate in Hong Kong, New York and Wolverhampton.

Cuddly-Shmuddly – a book on keeping and breeding unusual pets, including peacocks, skunks, anteaters, chameleons,[2] lobsters and sea cucumbers.

Hey Dummy! – a book on the use of plastic store-window mannequins in home decoration.

The Yorkie Man – a book on the trend towards writing books about trends (to be serialised in the *Tatler*).

The Truth About Jemima Puddleduck – a muck-raking exposé of the private lives of some of the classic authors of children's literature.

The Senator From Pinsk – a political thriller set in an alternative universe in which America declared war on the Soviet Union in 1946.

The following books are of a type to be avoided at all costs:

The Nice Woman – a critique of feminism which begins by quoting Dame Edith Evans: 'When a woman behaves like a man, why doesn't she behave like a nice man?'

Freebie! – a guide to getting things for free or at reduced prices.

Bobbysox to Stockings – advice for the parents of teenagers.

The Ramp Guide – a list of restaurants and nightclubs graded according to their accessibility for wheelchairs.

The Captain Beaky Cookbook[3]

---

[1] The Greaseman broadcasts on DC 101 Washington. His catch-phrase is 'hobbadegee'.

[2] Nimrod Bungle keeps a breeding pair which he calls 'Benson' and 'Hedges'.

[3] Not all birds are *ipso facto* sprezzless. In fact the sprezziest character in literature is Quacky-Jack (see *Josephine Goes Shopping* by Mrs H. C. Craddock).

Anything about AIDS, herpes, thrush, depression, obesity, transvestism or computers.

Probably the Best Lager in the World – a political thriller set in an alternative universe in which the Germans won the Second World War.

Finally, the *locus classicus* of non-sprezzy writing is *A World Apart* by Daphne Rae, the autobiography of a headmaster's wife. After the inevitable introduction by Lord Longford,[1] Mrs Rae launches into her own introduction, telling us how she gave the 'poorly typed' first draft to her husband and returned later to find him 'practically in tears with laughter'. '"You must get this printed," he laughed . . .'

------------------------------ **Poetry** ------------------------------

At the April meeting of the East Cannock Literary and Philosophical Society last year, Babs Phimister stunned everyone by reciting the following lines from the *Penguin Book of Contemporary Verse*:

> Now it is time to remember the winter festivals.
> He has gone down into the dark cellar.
> He drowsed and was aware of silence heaped,
> Ash on an old man's sleeve.
>
> Summer grows cold, cold-blooded mother,
> Dulled by the slow glare of the yellow bulb,
> The unpurged images of day recede.
> Now is the time for the burning of the leaves
> At the end of a long walled garden.
>
> He turned his field into a meeting place.
> O look how the loops and balloons of bloom

---

[1] 'I would rather be drowned than write a preface to any book whatsoever. Books should stand on their own feet . . . If they need shoring up by a preface here, an introduction there, they have no more right to exist than a table that needs a wad of paper under one leg in order to stand steady.' – Virginia Woolf.

Twined together and, as is customary,
The hop-poles stand in cones.

The valleys crack and burn, the exhausted plains
Beyond the edge of the sepia,
Lamps burn all the night,
Lovers whose lifted hands are candles in winter
More beautiful and soft than any moth.

Although I do not hope to turn again,
The lesson of our time is sore,
The oldest and simplest thoughts
In any medium except that of verse,
From fear to fear successively betrayed.

You must live through the time when everything hurts,
You that love England, who have an ear for her music.

Into the reverential silence which followed, Mrs Mortby, the vicar's wife, dropped the question, 'Who wrote that?'

'Sidney Keyes,' replied Babs, 'John Heath-Stubbs, Siegfried Sassoon, T. S. Eliot, Sylvia Plath, David Gascoyne, W. B. Yeats, Laurence Binyon, John Betjeman, W. H. Auden, W. R. Rodgers, Robert Graves, Edmund Blunden, Alun Lewis, Kenneth Allott, Patricia Beer, Anne Ridler, Stephen Spender, Charles Madge, Roy Fuller, Wyndham Lewis, William Empson and Cecil Day Lewis.'

'I don't understand,' said Mrs Mortby. 'You mean they *all* wrote it?'

'What I just read,' smiled Babs, 'was an edited version of the Index of First Lines. Didn't you realise?'

The May meeting was cancelled for lack of a quorum.

Music

It is important to own a collection of records which is either huge or tiny. I recommend that it should comprise either three LPs or more than 2,000.

To help you with the latter, Sprezzatura Enterprises can supply a set of twenty padlocked record-carrying cases, each capable of holding 100 albums or two bricks. Your record collection can go into the cases you leave unlocked.

If you choose the minimalist approach, it is advisable to own:
— one record by someone utterly obscure (Jumeaux Blon, the Cajun cellist, on the Flying Alligator label);
— one copy of something now forgotten, which was extremely unfashionable even when new ('Acker Bilk Plays Love Themes From the Movies');
— one record on which the ratio of surface noise to signal exceeds 2:1. (Leroy Carr's 'Black Snake Moan' is ideal. Or try 'Almost a Gentleman – The Music Hall Monologues of Billy Bennett').

If you are asked why you've only got three records, say either:
— 'I went mad last 18 September and smashed every-thing with a guitar on it.[1] then I cried for a week.'
— or 'I sold my collection to the Library Of Congress. Of course, I made them sign a covenant to keep it intact.'
— or 'I'm hoping to get down to two.'

When you are asked what sort of music you like, do *not* say, 'All sorts really', or 'Rock, country, you name it.' Say, 'Well at the moment I'm very interested in Melvin Carmody.[2] I've been listening a lot to his third album. (Pause) Side two, band four.'

If someone else is listing their likes, thus: 'Van Halen . . . ZZ Top . . . AC/DC . . .' you should add, with a nod and a smile, 'Whitesnake . . . Rush . . . Motorhead . . .'

Your victim will exclaim, 'Oh! We like the same music!' to which you reply:

'No, I was just completing the list for you.'

Updated lists of related performers are issued quarterly by Sprezzatura Enterprises. A mention of any one performer or group on a particular list allows you to mention all the others, secure in the knowledge that your victim will nod and smile happily at each. The lists should be memorised and destroyed. You do not get the same effect by reading them out.

---

[1] 18 September is the anniversary of Jimi Hendrix's death. Do not explain this unless asked.

[2] Any name will do, as long as it is both invented and unlikely.

How to sound sound on sound

Almost any sound system[1] can be made to seem impressive, except a music centre. If you own a music centre, sell it and spend £10 on a junk-shop Dansette (if possible the one with the cream vinyl cover with blue stars and the bronzed BSR autochange). You are entitled to describe this as 'the authentic sound of early-sixties rock'.

If you can stretch to a system of separate turntable, amplifier and speakers, however ill-assorted, proceed as follows:

1. Disconnect the leads from the turntable to the amplifier and from the amplifier to the speakers. You should plug them in (blowing vigorously on each connection) at the start of each record-playing session.

2. Remove the case from your amplifier. If it has valves rather than transistors, so much the better. On the front of the exposed chassis place a sticker that says 'DANGER – 5000 VOLTS' (Available from Sprezzatura Enterprises. 25p inc. p. & p.).

3. Take off the knobs. Adjustments to volume and tone should be made with a pair of pliers. You may choose to wear rubber gloves for this bit.

4. Say: 'The trouble with the amp I had before was that it wasn't built for this particular room.'

5. Wear white cotton gloves for handling records. The lowering of the pick-up on to the groove should take at least thirty seconds.

Lo-fi

If your sound system is audibly bad, you can turn the fact to your advantage. For example, you may choose to put both your tinny little speakers inside a large packing case or small wardrobe. Cut a 2-foot hole in the front and stretch hessian across it. Explain thus:

'It's an obsession a few of us have got. We like to recreate the authentic sound of the Wurlitzer Series Three Jukebox at maximum volume. I'd show you, but it hurts

---

[1] The preferred term. 'Hi-fi' and 'record-player' are terms to avoid. 'Gramophone' may be OK under certain circumstances, see 'Lo-fi' below.

your stomach muscles if you're not used to it.' Then play the music very quietly.

Alternatively, draw attention to the shortcomings of your system (that rattle on the bass notes . . . the dramatic turntable 'wow') by saying:

'Hear that? The rattle at three-fifty cycles? It's the authentic noise you got with equipment of the period.[1] Some people don't like it, but personally I don't think the music would sound right without it.' You may choose to add: 'You get it by putting a drawing pin in the speaker cone.'

When you are asked to admire someone else's expensive compact disc quadrophonic sound system, the following line of attack is strongly recommended:

— 'Your problem there is you're still using the ordinary domestic power supply.'
— 'Uh?'
— 'It makes me laugh really. People spend a fortune on all this elaborate gear, and then they plug it into the mains!'
— 'You have to, to make it work.'
— 'Quite.'

This should suffice. If pressed, however, continue as follows:

— 'What's the first thing you learn about electricity? A little rule called Ohm's Law. Resistance equals ampage over voltage.[2] Am I right?'
— 'Yes, but I don't see . . .'

You may now launch into any of a wide range of plonkingly obvious statements, such as:

— 'It's obvious. Electricity is carried by wires, right?'
or
— 'Sound is only a pattern of waves, right? That's all it is!'
or
— 'The man in charge of the power station is not thinking about your particular turntable, is he?'

---

[1] Don't say which period.
[2] Or is it voltage over ampage? No matter.

Tony Widgeon demonstrates his new sound system.

That should do the trick. In the unlikely event that you are asked to explain, you can launch thus (after a pause for 'thought'):

'Look. If you think of electricity as a long line of schoolboys, each with an orange in each hand . . . and each passes an orange to the boy in front and takes one from the boy behind . . .'

(The victim should by now be looking glazed. Or angry. Or better yet, both.)

'. . . Well what happens if one of the boys *drops his orange*?'

The only possible reply to this question is, 'How do you mean?'

You just shrug and smile. You win.

How to be a guitar star without actually learning to play

When you enter a room in which a guitar is casually displayed, DO NOT idly pick it up, strum chords C, D, D7 and back to C, then put it down again, being careful to avoid scratching the varnish. Do not, even worse, attempt to tune the thing. You will be marked at once as a beginner who never got past page four of Bert Weedon's *Teach Yourself To Play In A Day*.

The aim should be, rather, to convey the impression that this particular instrument is so cheap and nasty that it is beneath your dignity to play it.

Recommended ploys are:

— 'I like a guitar you can bend a bit. You can see this one's never been played. I'd probably snap the neck off.'

— 'If I play something like that it takes me a week to get any subtlety back in my left hand.'

— 'I couldn't play that. My little finger's not really strong enough.'[1]

— 'Have you *got* any beeswax?'[2]

A more sophisticated gambit is to carry with you a small plastic bag containing fifteen apparently identical plectrums. (The 'Plectrabag', available from Sprezzatura

---

[1] This sometimes provokes the counter: 'It gets stronger if you play a lot', to which the counter-counter is: 'Yes, but don't you find it wrecks the cartilage in your knuckle?'

[2] In the unlikely event that the answer is yes, ask, 'Austrian?'

Enterprises, £1.75 inc. VAT). Try out half a dozen (two plunks and discard). They will, of course, sound the same, but you should affect to hear subtle differences between the plunks. After much plunking, muttering and head-shaking, say apologetically,[1] 'I can't seem to find one to suit this particular instrument.'

Also available from Sprezzatura Enterprises:

The personalised record sleeve

Specially printed sleeves for certain selected classic rock albums, these are identical to the standard sleeve except that the list of musicians includes your own name. For example, 'Born in the USA' – Bruce Springsteen will feature the credit, 'Pedal steel guitar on "Cover Me" by (your name here).' There is, of course, no pedal steel on 'Cover Me'. This will not prevent people from hearing one.

Other titles now available:
Van Morrison – 'Beautiful Vision' (mandolin on 'Cleaning Windows')
Ry Cooder – 'Bop Till You Drop' (autoharp on 'Little Sister')
John Lennon – 'Rock 'n' Roll' (zither throughout)

The studio mixing chart

As all rock musicians know, the mixing chart is the sheet of paper which reminds the studio engineer which voices or instruments are on which tracks of a multitrack recording. Big studios use charts printed with their own logo, and Sprezzatura Enterprises can now supply forgeries of the charts used by:
Abbey Road Studios, London.
A. & R. Studios, New York.
Compass Point Studios, Nassau.
The Mongolian Hit Factory, Ulan Bator.
Having selected your chart, you should fill it in with the names of the musicians, thus:

L.VOC: TINA
B.VOC: ALF, LINDA, ARETHA

---

[1] But not *too* apologetically.

RTH GTR: KEEF
BASS: MACCA
DRMS: LEVON
SAX: LEE
PNO: JERRY
LEAD GTR: (Your name here, abbreviated if possible to a monosyllable. See the Sprezzatura Enterprises pamphlet, *Five Hundred Common Names With Their OK Abbreviations*.)

Leave the chart lying about. If anyone expresses interest in it, say: 'Oh Christ, that's supposed to be a secret!'

————————— **Photography** —————————

Taking photographs is non-sprezzy. This is partly because no one can afford the sort of equipment that makes a photographer look unmistakably professional, partly because even a professional photographer is no longer an impressive thing to be,[1] and partly for the reasons outlined by Susan Sontag in her book *On Photography*.

Miss Sontag's argument, in essence, is that the reason the Americans and the Japanese take so many photographs is because their national characters are imbued with the work ethic; they are incapable of enjoying leisure and therefore they turn their holidays into an occupation, measuring their success in terms of productivity — so many places seen, so many rolls of film exposed. All of which, I need hardly say, is the antithesis of sprezz.

If someone else insists on taking photographs, however, there is not much you can do about it except submit to being snapped. To conceal your face is to risk looking like a murder suspect on the way to the police station.

The following poses are acceptably sprezzy:

Laughing wildly at something, unaware of the camera.
Looking down and to the right with a bored expression.
Seen through a car window, preferably in the rain.
Seen from behind.

---

[1] A classic case of a profession's public image becoming so enviable (*Blow Up*, Lichfield, etc.) that everyone refuses to believe it and insists that, on the contrary, photographers have a thoroughly rotten time.

Whereas these poses are to be avoided:

Smiling at the camera.
Looking soulfully at the camera.
In three-quarter profile looking 'intelligent'.
Sticking your tongue out (especially at a fish-eye lens, a favourite early Johnny Rotten pose).
Shaking hands with someone more famous than you are.
With a dog, cat or vase of flowers.
In a bathing costume.[1]

Clothes

As soon as one considers the problem of dress, one is back in the thickets of the class system (see chapter 1). Paul Fussell has offered us the formula: 'The sloppier the bow-tie, the higher the class' and there is much in what he says. He goes on: 'The upper classes like to appear in old clothes, as if to advertise how much of conventional dignity they can afford to throw away, e.g. wearing loafers without socks.' Which is all very well, provided you can be absolutely sure that your socklessness will be perceived as an eccentric whim rather than as evidence of either poverty or a nasty fungus infection.

In the end it is for each sprezzperson to evolve his or her own dress-style, guided by the three alternative approaches outlined at the beginning of this chapter. The first of these ('My taste is better than yours') is one I recommend only with some diffidence. For those who would take the higher path in matters of fashion, the way is perilous and steep, and so are the prices. You have to be able to afford designer clothes and to wear them without looking silly.[2] Sewing designer labels in chain store garments never works (if anyone is going to be fooled by it, the designer name won't mean anything to them anyway). For most of us, keeping up with serious fashion is a non-option. Besides, fashion, according to

---

[1] Adolf Hitler said, 'If he wishes to be taken seriously no statesman should ever be photographed in a bathing suit'. (One suspects that there was more to Hitler's rise to power than that, but it is a useful beginning.)
[2] c.f. Joan Collins.

Hazlitt, is 'gentility running away from vulgarity and afraid of being overtaken', and to the extent that fashion is unrelaxed it is correspondingly unsprezzy.

The second approach, based on kitsch, has more to recommend it. The following outfit, sported by Wincey Bollard at the wedding of her sister Coriander to Jock Matumbe, is, I think, definitive:

see-through pink plastic mac
wooden tie with pokerwork nude
tee-shirt with picture of dill pickle and slogan: 'Greenblatts – estd. 1926. The wine merchant that fronts as a deli'
moleskin trousers
silver platform-soled boots (ex-Dave Hill, lead guitarist with Slade)
leopardskin pillbox hat.

The total effect was stunning.

Seriously though, it comes down, doesn't it, to good old Parton's Pleasure?

'One must be correct, yes, but the correctness must be instinctive, inbred. One must not try, because effort was common. In fact one must go to the other extreme, make efforts to be anti-effort.'

Thus Nik Cohn, in his book *Today There Are No Gentlemen*, describes the pre-war attitude to male fashion. And this, I submit, is the most appropriate attitude to clothes for the sprezzperson of today.

The aim, then, is to be conservative without dowdiness; to imply a lack of concern for one's appearance which is both reassuring ('This person is not in competition with me . . .') and at the same time deeply threatening ('. . . so how come he/she looks so good, dammit?'); to be the worst-dressed person in the room, and somehow make everyone else feel overdressed.

A perfectly acceptable substitute for dieting is a stout corset, but it must be tightly laced. Gravity can help.

TEST PAPER

Section A

1. Which of the following *objets trouvés* would you accord a place in your living room?

a. Glass case containing stuffed kittens dressed as a wedding party.

b. Mauretanian camel saddle.

c. Cardboard box containing 500 Pan-American Airways sickbags.

d. Empty whisky bottle labelled 'Mississippi John Hurt. 28.10.66.'

2. If you had to choose only one design of Christmas card to send to all your friends and acquaintances (if any), would it be:

a. A home-made card featuring a fuzzy potato-cut of a plum pudding?

b. A tasteful Oxfam job with a non-denominational seasonal greeting in four languages?

c. A Woolworths stagecoach-in-the-snow number?

d. A picture postcard of the ruins of Ankor Wat?

3. You have borrowed from the library a copy of *H. G. Wells and Rebecca West* by Gordon N. Ray, chapter ten of which begins: 'The winter of 1922/3 passed without special incident . . .' Do you scribble in the margin:

a. 'Indeed?!!'?

b. 'NB Must write and tell him about Nadia and the spats.'?

c. 'Unless you count a General Election, the discovery of Tutankhamun's tomb and the establishment of the USSR!'?

4. (This question is for men and certain kinds of women.) At a party, someone admires your Marks and Spencers shirt. Do you say:
a. 'There's only one man in this country who knows how to cut a shirt, and that's Mario at *Mister Poopie's.*'
b. 'I got it off a New York wino for twenty Chesterfield and a pair of earmuffs.'
c. 'It's bloody awful, actually, but I had to borrow it off Gerry cos I was sick down the one I came in.'

5. What is the correct answer to the question, 'Do you write poetry?'
a. 'Nothing original, I'm afraid, but I have translated most of the Old Norse sagas into rhyming couplets.'
b. 'Yes. As a matter of fact I'm planning to start a new poem in March.'
c. 'No. I make it up and commit it to memory.'
d. 'Nothing you're likely to have come across.'

Section B (Open-ended questions)

1. If the spice rack in your kitchen had ten slots, which ten spices would you put in it (assuming you were never going to use any of them)?

2. Culture, according to T. S. Eliot, consists of 'all the characteristic activities and interests of a people. Derby Day, Henley Regatta, Cowes, the 12th of August, a cup final, the dog races, the pin table, the dartboard, Wensleydale cheese, boiled cabbage cut into sections, beetroot in vinegar, 19th century Gothic churches, the music of Elgar . . .'
Choose three items from this list and demonstrate, using diagrams if necessary, that each of them is more important than Shakespeare.

3. Explain why *Pink String and Sealing Wax*, starring Googie Withers, is the best British film ever made.

Now check your score

Section A

1. *a* – wrong (Why keep them in a glass case? Take them out and spread them around.)
   b – wrong (Are you any good at camel stories? Yes, well you may think so, but I doubt it frankly.)
   c – wrong (Why would anyone want *that* in their living room?)
   d – only as part of a collection. Score two.
2. *a, b* and *c* are too subtle by half. *d* is OK if you can arrange to have the cards posted in Bangkok. Score three.
3. *b* and *c* are over-elaborate. *a* is nice and simple, but do you really need two exclamation marks? Score three.
4. *a* is precious, *c* is yobbish and *b* is a bit early-seventies. Take your pick. Score five if you refused to answer.

5. *a, b* and *c* are vulnerable to counters. *d* is safe and
   incorporates a neat put-down. Score five.

Section B

1. Score one point for each spice on the following list:
   saffron, coriander, whole cloves, nutmeg, turmeric,
   tarragon, cinnamon (sticks, not ground), garam
   masala, rosemary, oregano.
   If you included three or more jars of any one of these,
   score five.
   Deduct one point for minced garlic, ground ginger or
   barbecue seasoning. Deduct five points for curry
   powder.

5

THE DEEPER THINGS

*Well, it's all been very interesting
– last words of*
Lady Mary Wortley-Montagu

I suppose it is possible that some of my readers may have opinions. I do not want to discourage them, but they should accept that, for sprezz purposes, deeply held views are at best unhelpful and at worst disastrous. It is your role, as sprezzperson, to be a moral gadfly.

Your adversaries will be of two kinds: plonkers and ditherers. The plonker has a point of view and asserts it at every opportunity. Your approach here will be Socratic, teasing out ever-more-extreme statements, each logically implied by its predecessor, until your victim is trapped in a palpable absurdity. The ditherer, on the other hand, is impressed by sheer force of argument, particularly if the ideas you express are off-beat or extreme, and even more so if they appear to have been plucked out of thin air.

In neither case should you ever make a statement which reflects your sincerely held opinion, if any; it restricts your room for manoeuvre.[1]

---

[1] Pincus takes a contrary view on this aspect of sprezz theory (although whether he believes it is anyone's guess). He argues that the sprezziest moment in the life of Bertrand Russell occurred in September 1919: Philip Jourdain, the Cambridge mathematician, lay dying. On his deathbed he became obsessed with the notion that he had found a new proof of the multiplicative axiom. He begged Russell to come and see him about it, but Russell refused, on the grounds that, even for the sake of a dying man, it could never be right to entertain arguments incompatible with mathematical truth. Sprezzy certainly, but how does Pincus know that Russell actually gave a damn?

If you can't be sure, be obscure. So runs the ancient sprezzrule. In other words, one of the best ways to win an argument is to say something which sounds terribly wise and profound, but which nobody quite understands. Here is Francine Spong in conversation with Charles Buskitt:

Charles   All I'm saying is that equality of opportunity, if it's to mean anything, has to begin with the home environment, not just with society's educational provision . . .

Francine   You can't run a racing car on bread and butter pudding, Charles.

Charles   No, I suppose not. (THINKS: 'Eh?')

Which brings us to the instant aphorism.

Instant Aphorisms

Convincing Rumanian and Armenian proverbs can be made to order by mixing and matching items from the following lists. Example: 'Better a thousand fleabites than an arrow in the neck.'

BETTER

a sip of plum brandy
a door without a lock
a slap on the back
a barking dog
a mad woman
a cart with no wheels
a wedding in Odessa
a priest's belly

THAN

a day without whistling
waiting for sunset
a pocketful of fish-hooks
a camel with no tail
a mouldy yoghurt
a picture of the Tsar's dinner
a mother-in-law's advice on etiquette
a hole in the roof

95

Alternatively:

> THE
>
> bee
> peasant
> donkey
> king
> fish
> house
> old woman
> sheep
> ocean
>
> SAID TO THE
>
> cormorant
> soil
> crying child
> spinning wheel
> peppercorn
> garden
> flower-seller
> bucket
> tax-collector
>
> 'There is not enough water'
> 'Your neck is too long'
> 'Sugar is sweeter than milk'
> 'A blanket with holes makes a better coat than
> one without'
> 'Without paper there would be no wars'
> 'Umbrellas only work when it's raining'
> 'A hen is only an egg's way of making another
> egg'
> 'A tree can make many window-frames, but a
> window is sad without a tree
> outside it'
> 'Every fire is hotter than it needs to be'

Having mastered the basics of constructing instant aphorisms in this colour-by-numbers way, why not move on to designing and building them to your own patterns? Here are some thoughts to start you off:

Life is the process by which a can of strawberries gets

wrongly labelled as rhubarb and so turns sour before it is opened.

('Life is . . .' is always a good beginning.)

Love without kissing is dehydrated water.

The road to success is paved with dropped bollocks.

Religion

When two or three sprezzpeople are gathered together, all religious argument inevitably boils down to atheism versus the Church of England.[1] This illustrates the crucial point that debate is most fruitful when the opposed views are so close as to be almost identical.

Atheism can be sprezzy, but only if you make the clearest possible distinction between your own philosophy[2] and the soap-box assertions of the scientific rationalists (small men with raincoats and moustaches who witter on about the dreadful deeds of the Spanish Inquisition). You might like to hint at a Roman Catholic upbringing and a traumatic loss of faith brought on by either a visit to Ecuador, the abolition of the Latin Mass, or watching the play of light on the surface of a wet cowpat.

Exotic religions have always sold well, but Buddhism (Straight, Tantric and Zen), Hinduism, Druidism, Islam, Born-again Christian Evangelism, Judaism, Spiritualism, Rosicrucianism and Rastafarianism were all pretty thoroughly done in the sixties and seventies, several of them by Bob Dylan alone. There is still mileage in one or two of the oriental religions, notably Taoism and Shinto, but for the late eighties we are currently recommending Primitive Spirit Animism (in three varieties, Red Indian, Eskimo and West African Tribal).

The idea is that everything – a table, a hammer, a Swiss cheese plant, a pebble, a Volkswagen Golf GTi – has a soul and a spirit-force. The notion of saying a little prayer to the video-recorder ('Please switch on at the right time and record the right channel, amen') or making a small but heartfelt blood sacrifice to the central heating boiler ('I destroy this earwig in your honour, oh mighty thunder-

---

[1] Not which is truer, of course, but which is sprezzier.

[2] Existential angst is the mood to aim at, but don't call it that.

er . . .') may strike you as quaint, but as a practical expression of the religious urges of twentieth-century Western suburbia, Animism has a lot to recommend it.

If you're going to be C of E and have done with it, *you must not discuss your beliefs*. Religious conversation among Sprezzanglicans takes the form of cosy chats about the need for new hassocks in the choir stalls, the supply of ham rolls for the Brownie picnic and the hostess rota for the famine-relief coffee mornings during Lent. Any questions which seek to probe deeper than this should be answered, 'Well that sort of thing is strictly speaking ineffable.'

All of which leaves unanswered the question, 'What do you do when attacked by a religious bore?' Here are a few strategies:

Bore	Do you know Jesus?
Sprezzperson	We're certainly not on first-name terms.
Bore	It's more or less conclusively proved that primitive man was visited by alien beings from space, so actually all religion is based on worshipping flying saucers . . .
Sprezzperson	It would be nice to think so. A neat explanation of the supernatural elements in religious dogma would paradoxically reinforce the moral content of spiritual teaching, but of course this was all sorted out in the eleventh century.
Bore	I don't believe in God, necessarily, but I regard myself as a Christian. In fact I reckon I'm a better Christian than a lot of people who do believe in God.
Sprezzperson	Listen everybody, Eric's doing this amazing impression of the Bishop of Durham . . .

Bore	I just think Jesus was a fantastically great guy, that's all.
Sprezzperson	Sure, but where does that leave eschatology?

Politics

Political arguments start in many different ways, but they all resolve themselves after a while into ritual sniping from entrenched positions.

The following brief questionnaire will tell you everything you need to know about your political opinions:

1. Do you start by:
   a. deciding where you want to go?
   b. looking at where you are?
   c. taking a vote?
2. When things go wrong, is it because of:
   a. a conspiracy?
   b. a cock-up?
   c. bad luck?
3. Are people basically:
   a. good but stupid?
   b. bad but smart?
   c. OK?
4. Is the situation:
   a. hopeless?
   b. tolerable?
   c. worrying?

Now check your score. Mostly *a* – You are a revolutionary, possibly a Marxist, possibly a radical Conservative ('fascist' to those who disagree). Mostly *b* – You are an old-fashioned Tory with SDP leanings. Mostly *c* – You are a humanitarian socialist or a wishy-washy liberal do-gooder.

The advantage of knowing about these four crucial tests is that it allows you to short-circuit any political argument. For example:

Peabody	(IN MID-DRONE) The revisionists in the Soviet Union and elsewhere have betrayed the basic principles of Marxism–Leninism whereby Lenin

	said that after the revolution bureaucrats should be paid at the same rate as ordinary workers, whereas the differential in Russia today is about thirty-to-one, so you've got rampant careerism . . .
Node	Yes, but what you call class-compromise is actually a perception that society is a single organic structure which will only develop if everyone's self-interest drives them towards a collective goal . . .
Sprezzperson	(INTERRUPTING) It seems to me that the argument between you is simply this: Peabody believes people are good but stupid, whereas you think they're bad but smart.
Peabody	Erm . . .
Node	Ah . . .

————Hangers and Floggers————

Even people who don't drive taxis occasionally argue that soccer hooligans should be birched and that when it comes to child-murderers, IRA bombers and heroin-pushers, 'hanging's too good for the bastards'.

It is a mistake to try to argue rationally with these folk. You can always agree with them (even if you share their opinions) but that doesn't score you many points. The way to tackle them (and it can equally be applied to racists, hardline male chauvinists, religious bigots and Barry Manilow fans) is as follows:

| Flogger | What they want to do with them Millwall supporters, they want to send the police in with teargas and rubber bullets. Soon sort 'em out, the bastards . . . |
| Sprezzperson | Tell me, when were you first |

	aware of having these strong feelings about football fans?
Flogger	I dunno. You didn't get all this violence when I was a lad. Now in those days, if you raised your hand to a copper . . .
Sprezzperson	So was there a particular incident that made you angry – perhaps hurt you deeply as a *person*?
Flogger	Did you see that in the paper about the bastards throwing darts at people? Nearly blinded one poor sod . . .
Sprezzperson	So it's really to do with a deep-seated fear of darts, or dart-shaped objects?
Flogger	It's not the darts, it's those bastards . . .
Sprezzperson	A *repressed* fear of dart-shaped objects. That would tie in with the rubber bullets, of course. Tell me, were you sexually molested at all, as a child?
Flogger	Was I buggery!
Sprezzperson	Now why, I wonder, do you instinctively choose that form of words?

The Occult

A cynical point of view on matters occult and paranormal would appear to be sound sprezz-play, but it can leave you looking a bit of a boring old sod. If you're going to claim that spoon-bending is a fraud, it helps to be able to do a couple of conjuring tricks to demonstrate the fact. Moreover, the 'sceptical sniff' strategy is always vulnerable to attack from the scientifically clued-up plonker who uses the 'weird things happening at the frontiers of research' approach, thus:

Sceptic	Psychology teaches us that if something extraordinary appears to be going on,

it is far more likely to be a distortion of our perception than a breach of the laws of nature . . .

Plonker	But what about the behaviour of subatomic particles in a linear accelerator?
Sceptic	Even so . . .
Plonker	You know the experiment I'm referring to?
Sceptic	It's a long way from subatomic particles to a theory of telepathy or . . .
Plonker	The equations exist, dammit!
Sceptic	No doubt, but . . . that is to say . . .

No, the only safe line on the paranormal is 'open-minded without being gullible'. Do not confuse this with the 'all a bit of fun' approach, which puts you on very shaky ground indeed, thus:

Funster	I had my palm read once by a seaside clairvoyant, just for a giggle. She told me I'd be married twice and I'd probably suffer with back trouble, ha ha.
Gloombonnet	Have you told your husband?
Funster	Yes, we both laughed about it.
Gloombonnet	It's not a thing to giggle about. These things are often better kept to yourself. It's possible that these predictions work through autosuggestion but we know too little about it. Have you in fact had back trouble?
Funster	I get a twinge now and then . . .
Gloombonnet	Do you still love your husband? Does he still love you?
Funster	Yes, of course.
Gloombonnet	Hm. If it was a divorce she'd probably have said so. It begins to look like a sudden death, doesn't it?

| *Funster* | Ooh, don't be morbid. It was only a bit of fun. |
| *Gloombonnet* | All I can say is that you have a curious idea of fun. |

Astrology

Study the following dialogue:

A What sign is he?
B His sun is in Libra.
A Funny, I wouldn't have said Libra.
B Of course you wouldn't. He's obviously earth-cardinal. But he's got a Sun–Saturn conjunct absolutely spot-on in the first decanate, with everything else[1] in a 120-degree bundle Cancer to Scorpio. Except Jupiter, and you can guess where that is.
A Where?
B Aries. Opposing the Sun–Saturn conjunct. It's absolutely classic. No trines. No sextiles apart from the usual one.
A (Rallying bravely) So it's no wonder he went off with Sarah . . .
B No, that's his Venus–Mars conjunct square Neptune. He does it every time there's a transit.
A (Reduced to pathetic punning) Better keep him away from vans then, eh?
B wins by a sniff.

The point is, you can learn all the jargon in ten minutes. If you want to use it correctly (not that anyone will know the difference) you may need to spend a little longer than that with one of the standard texts. But balance that against the time you've already wasted listening to dumbos at parties wittering on about always being able to spot a Virgo ho ho, and you will see that it's worth the small effort.

---

[1] Randy Waxheimer, Californian astro-sprezzer, uses the phrase 'all the rest of the shit' to describe heavenly bodies not specifically itemised.

——————————Vegetarianism——————————

There is a paradox here. Whereas it is entirely sprezzy to be a[1] vegetarian, it is extremely unsprezzy to announce the fact without being asked. If you arrive at a dinner party and are served meat, simply transfer it delicately to your side-plate and eat the vegetables.

To make a big deal of your meat-free existence is to invite retribution in a variety of forms, from the crass ('A vegan, eh? No wonder you've got pointed ears . . .') to the spuriously scientific ('Did you know that scientists can now measure the pain suffered by a radish being pulled out of the ground? Apparently, allowing for the difference in size, it's equivalent to what an elephant would suffer if you put it in a car-crushing machine.')

When guests ring Mary Limkin to tell her of their vegetarianism, she ignores the warnings and serves them meat anyway. Most are too embarrassed to complain, but to those who do she replies:

'Vegetarian? I thought you said Sagittarian! I made a point of serving steak au poivre because your ruling planet is in Taurus at the moment . . .'

——————————Feminism——————————

Militant feminism is a tricky attitude for the male to counter. The bluff, hearty 'Call me a chauvinist pig if you like but . . .' approach has serious limitations. Your adversary undoubtedly *will* call you a chauvinist pig, and you'll be left looking slightly pathetic in the eyes of both your friends and hers. Provided you don't look or sound remotely homosexual, it is suggested that you try the McBurge Overkill Strategy.

Far from opening doors for women, Cecil McBurge tends to slam doors in their faces. Here he is in action against Nancy Finniston. Observe that liberation does little to alter woman's essential gullibility:

---

[1] 'A vegetarian' rather than just 'vegetarian'. The noun is sprezzier than the adjective.

Nancy	(In full flood) Just because I try to make myself look attractive, it doesn't mean I'm inviting men to harass me sexually.
Cecil	I don't think you *do* look attractive. I think it's an insult to suggest such a thing.
Nancy	Well . . . yes. It is.
Cecil	In fact I hadn't actually noticed your gender until you mentioned it.
Nancy	How d'you mean?
Cecil	It doesn't matter. Would it help to tell me about it?
Nancy	About what?
Cecil	About your bad experiences with men.
Nancy	Erm . . .
Cecil	Don't be afraid to be really bitter.
Nancy	I dunno. Some men can be OK really.
Cecil	OK? OK? Define your terms. OK in what way?
Nancy	Like I knew one guy who . . . well, when I had a tummy-bug he went to the launderette for me.
Cecil	Oh my Goddess! Really! I could weep for you if it weren't for my macho conditioning in infancy – something I'm deeply ashamed of by the way. You've been brainwashed too, haven't you?
Nancy	I suppose . . . I dunno . . .
Cecil	This bloke – wasn't there anything he did that made you livid?
Nancy	He didn't always put the top back on the toothpaste.
Cecil	What a swine! What a slob! Men like that make me sick! Perhaps you'd better tell me the whole story.
Nancy	All right. Maybe I could buy you dinner and we'll talk about it.
Cecil	Fine. Pick me up about eight.

The more aggressive feminist can be a pain to women as well as to men. Deirdre Peasmire has devised this elegant shutting-up technique:

Feminist   (In full flood) I never wear a watch. I think punctuality is a male concept. Men run their lives by the clock, but women follow the cycles of the moon, the tides and the seasons . . .

Deirdre   Look, you're obviously a keen feminist. Perhaps you'd like to join our nude-in?

Feminist   What's a nude-in?

Deirdre   It's a protest demonstration against the sexual politics of pornography. The idea is, we all go down to the British Legion on stag night, and then when the stripper comes on, we all take our clothes off, as an act of solidarity and sisterhood. It's very very meaningful. I mean, sometimes you can see that the men are deeply moved in spite of themselves. Tears come to their eyes.

Feminist   Erm . . . well . . . I dunno . . .

Deirdre   I mean it's so easy to talk about male domination, yet how many women ever go out and do something about it? Hm?

(Feminist goes very quiet)

Travel

Travel is sprezzy; tourism is not. If you can't compete with the globe-trotters, you should beware of the self-excusing whine ('We've sacrificed our holidays to give the children a private education') or the utterly pathetic ('A friend of mine went to Hong Kong last year. I believe it's very nice').

There is something to be said for, 'When I was there twenty years ago it was quite unspoiled. I imagine it's hell on earth these days,' a comment which can be applied to virtually anywhere except Blackpool. But for sheer dis-missiveness the prize goes to Ivy Compton-Burnett who hated abroad so much that she not only never went there, she also kept a blacklist of people who lived there.

If you choose to compete for the Happy Wanderer Challenge Trophy, you will need either a lot of money and spare time or a broad streak of cunning. Exotic holidays can be simulated in retrospect; for example, rather than pay for a trip to the Mardi Gras, debit your account for the following:

— a course of sunbed sessions.
— a visit to the Tropical House at Kew, where you can be photographed in medium close-up against a background of frangipanis.
— a second-hand trombone in a battered case (paint 'Jazzbo Wilkins' on the lid).
— a New Orleans street map (so you can memorise and subsequently describe in detail how to get from Bienville Street onto State Highway 23 for Breton Sound).
— a large bottle of Jack Daniels sourmash whisky.
— a recipe for gumbo stew taken from the *Ladies' Home Journal* (order this through your local newsagent) and copied in drunken handwriting onto the inner sleeve of an import Professor Longhair and his Shuffling Hungarians LP.
— a marabou feather dyed pink.

Skiing holidays are even cheaper to simulate; they amount to an elastic bandage and a larger-than-usual pair of goggles for the sunbed sessions.

You will want to know how to deal with the sort of travel bores who talk about 'Barthelona'. One option is to send them up mercilessly by describing a visit to a Spanish 'humble-sale', but I rather like the opposite technique of being terribly English. Don't say *vinho verde*, say 'green wine'. Come out with lines like, 'We went to this delightful little . . . what would one call it in English? . . . *bodega*? . . . I suppose you'd call it a sort of cellar-bar . . .'

The Tostages from Bromley (Richard and Helen) were particularly irritating because they would come back from a fortnight in Crete, take us to a Greek restaurant and address the waiter in his native tongue. Phil Bixham put a stop to it by saying, 'Look Richard, I hope you don't mind my pointing out that, using that particular Iraklian accent, you're coming across as a sort of Greek equivalent of John Inman.'

Richard got his own back the following year, when the Tostages returned from Ibiza and he told us a long anecdote about a wrangle over the villa's septic tank, switching halfway through into a stream of Spanish ('*Todas las connexiones al panel posterior se efectuarán estando apagados todos los aparatos. Para evitar confusiones, conecte en una misma operación un cable entre los diferentes elementos del equipo. Es la manera más segura de evita confusiones de canales y de entradas con salidas*') which, as he later admitted to me privately, he had memorised from the multilingual instruction leaflet for his Maranz radio tuner.[1]

---

[1] 'All connections to the rear panel should be made with the power to the entire system turned off. To avoid confusion, connect one cable at a time between the different components of your system. This is the safest way to avoid cross-connecting channels or confusing signal inputs with outputs.'

TEST PAPER

Section A

1. Which of the following lines would you use to escape from a bore?

a. 'I usually say a few prayers at this time of day. Perhaps you'd care to join me?'

b. 'Let me leave you with an epistemological conundrum: If Helen Keller fell down in the forest, would she make a sound?'

c. 'I do hope you'll forgive me, but I've just heard that my house is on fire. I wouldn't mind, but it's a part of St James's Palace.'[1]

2. Conversation turns to the forthcoming budget. Do you remark:

a. 'I've ordered a couple of cases of Glenlivet at the current price, just in case.'?

b. 'I'm one of those maddening people who don't mind paying income tax. I regard it as a privilege.'?

c. 'Redistribution of wealth is all very well, but as Shaw pointed out, if you abolished all the millionaires and shared out their money, we'd get sixpence each.'?

3. As the only woman present among a group of men, how would you answer the statement, 'These women's libbers are either too ugly to pull a feller, or they're lesbians anyway'?

a. 'What is it about feminism that you find *most* threatening?'

---

[1] Sir Michael Adeane to Basil Boothroyd.

b. 'I suppose all homosexuals are inclined to be hostile to the opposite sex.'

c. 'Which am I, would you say?'

4. A friend remarks that since she took up meditation she has achieved total inner contentment. How do you reply?

a. 'You know, there's an Armenian proverb: to seek contentment in life is to wish for death.'

b. 'That's marvellous. In fact the only place I've seen a smile like yours was on the face of a lice-ridden beggar in a Bombay gutter, just before he was run over by a bus.'

c. 'Yes, everyone feels that when they first start. Then after a while you learn to accept suffering. It's not as pleasant as the initial stages, but you'll find it's much more rewarding.'

5. You are asked whether you've ever been to a seance. Do you reply:

a. 'No, but I've dabbled in necromancy. We conjured up a fairly low-grade demon and ordered it to torment Ian Paisley.'?

b. 'Yes. The medium reckoned she was in contact with the spirit of a Victorian milkmaid, but when I asked her about cheese-making, she hadn't a clue.'?

c. 'Not on this plane, but my astral body has attended several.'?

Section B (Open-ended questions)

1. Given a budget of £25, how would you simulate a holiday in Micronesia?

2. Analyse the philosophical difficulties
   implied by the question: If truth is
   beauty, how come no one has their hair
   done in the library? (Tomlin)

3. Argue that all human life is part of a
   ceaseless struggle between the forces of
   light and darkness. Illustrate your answer
   with references to the Top Forty.

Now check your score

1. *a* and *b* will do at a pinch, but *c* is clearly superior if
   you can make it believable. Score five.

2. *a* looks mean, *b* sounds pompous and *c* is a touch
   banal. Choose the one most suited to your own
   character (Everybody's either mean, pompous or
   banal. Of course they are.) and score three.

3. *a* is correct sprezzplay; score two. *b* is unworthy. *c* is
   excellent, but only if there is no possibility of the reply
   'Both'. Score five.

4. *a* is wrong. Armenian proverbs have to mention
   animals or kitchen utensils. *b* and *c* both score three;
   the difference is that for *c* you have to look earnest,
   which some people find difficult.

5. *a* could be a joke or it could be serious. If you can
   preserve this ambiguity in your delivery of the line,
   score three. *b* is a bit prosaic but could form part of a
   sustained rationalist plonk; score two. *c* is just silly;
   score ten.

About to go to a party with his friend Fermage, Jonathan 'The Killer' Mottershead demonstrates, with diagrams, the importance of checking underarm hygiene.

SPREZZATURA AND THE SOCIAL OCCASION

If God would give thee grace to see yoursel' as ithers see ye, ye would throw your dinner up.
R. L. Stevenson

A party may pretend to be a recreational gathering of friends and acquaintances, a social function designed to promote relaxation and the enjoyment of food, drink, music and conversation; but we know, don't we, that it's really a battlefield. It's the classic opportunity to polish your own credibility and shred everybody else's.

It is universally agreed that two people cannot be in the same room for five minutes without one of them establishing superiority over the other. Where fifty people are in the same room it just takes longer for a clear pecking-order to emerge; usually about twelve minutes.

At any party the guest has this advantage over the host: that the guest has only his own credibility to concern him, while the host is bound to worry also lest he be judged by the company he keeps. There is not much consolation in being thought an ace face if it is also considered that your friends are a bunch of bums. I have known a host be so ashamed of the rabble who turned up at his party that he pretended to be a gatecrasher and lurched about asking pathetically where he could find the bog.

There are two chief rules for the prospective host to

bear in mind. They were laid down in a Victorian manual of etiquette[1] in these words:

> 'Avoid acting as host to wordly persons who are richer than yourself. They rarely make allowances and are prone to make unkind remarks.'
> and
> 'You should never perplex your soul by striving to amuse your guest. Give him some credit for resources within himself.'

In the opening phase of the campaign, the central problem for the party-giver is this: how do you issue an invitation to someone without conveying the unfortunate implication that you value their company? It is difficult, but it *can be managed*. Here are four suggestions:

'Nothing Unusual'

You seek to give the impression that every night is party night round at your place. The atmosphere of impromptu celebration — the 'spur of the moment' approach — can be cultivated by, for example, waiting until most of the guests have arrived before 'nipping to the offy' for the drink. The food may, if you wish, be delicious, but it should take no longer than five minutes to produce from freezer, tin or packet.[2]

There will, of course, be no glasses or plates, and any attempt at 'inducing an atmosphere' should be limited to the discreet removal of the odd fuse from the fusebox, so that when the lights don't work you can laughingly produce a stub of candle. (Be careful not to remove power from the record-player, or someone may laughingly produce a guitar, harmonica or — God help us — penny-whistle, and then you're sunk.)

Invitations to this sort of party should be given by hand, no more than forty-eight hours ahead, and should be written in biro on the inner surface of a split beermat.

---

[1] *You Should: A Manual, brief and simple, of Hints and Instructions for Men and Women* by 'Nod', p. 1884 London.

[2] See the Sprezzatura Enterprises leaflet, *A Hundred Party Recipes That Look Like Leftover Breakfast*, and (in preparation) *How To Make Chinese Takeaways In Your Own Kitchen*.

'The Social Experiment'

Your role is not so much host as sociologist. The aim is to suggest that you (moving effortlessly as you do through the social range) are putting together some people who may just 'react interestingly'. The nice thing about this ploy is that whatever happens you can't lose.

If the party is a success, you've proved a theory about the breaking down of class/age/cultural divisions; or, as you will no doubt choose to put it as you wish your guests goodnight: 'I had an idea that 28 per cent second-generation lower C and D-plus backgrounds would interact nicely with about 35 per cent of people . . . well, like you and Joan.'

If the party is a failure and leads to violence or, even worse, glassy-eyed boredom, you can always say: 'Well, so much for the Stickford and Willis theory on the politico-cultural split. There just weren't enough random factors. Actually, Tom, I was expecting you to be more of a catalyst than you were, but you probably felt inhibited by Monica's textbook approach to the interactive sequences.'

Finally, if everyone who comes is precisely the same age, social class and political outlook as everyone else, you can explain that this party is merely the control group. The real experiment is happening next Saturday and *they're not invited*.

'Third Division'

Your invitation includes the line: 'We're having a series of parties to let people see our new house' (This after you've been there at least eighteen months, implying that at the rate of fifty people a month, it's taken quite a while to get round to these creeps).

A slightly more complicated variant is to send an invitation which gives five alternative dates, inviting your guest to 'tick the most convenient day on the tear-off portion below, and return within seven days'. This allows you to choose a day for your party which will give the fewest possible guests the option of using that deadly line: 'Sorry I couldn't make it.' It also allows you to include in your invitation to everyone who chose a different date the delightful put-down: 'Sorry I couldn't fit you in on the eleventh as you asked, but everyone seemed to want that

day, so I've had to move a few to the 18th. Hope you
don't mind too much . . .'

'The Gatsby'

You throw a glittering party *which you do not yourself
attend*. This move is unbeatable.

INVITATIONS

WRONG

236 5621

The Rodings,[1]
Greenford.

2nd Dec.

Dear *Harold*[2]

Marjorie and I are having a
few people in for drinks[3] on
the evening of the 23rd.
You might care to come along.

Jeremy.

P.S. Bring Judith[4] if you like.

259.[5]

---

[1] Note imprecise address. Guest will have to ring for directions, and to ask what time to come. This avoids your writing 'R.S.V.P.', implying as it does that you care either way.

[2] The guest's name, the P.S. and (optionally) your own signature are handwritten. The rest of the letter is a rather fuzzy xerox copy.

[3] 'A few people in for drinks' covers up to 200 guests. Over 200, the formula is 'some friends round for the evening'.

[4] His wife's name is, of course, Janet.

[5] Number your invitations, starting from 250.

When addressing party invitations, write Ann for Anne, Clare for Claire, Jackie for Jacqui, Jon for John, Sara for Sarah, Steven for Stephen and vice versa.[1]

The business of accepting a party invitation is comparatively straightforward. There are only two recommended poses:

'How Badly Do You Need Me?'

Suggest that if it is going to help, you are prepared to put back the Los Angeles trip and risk offending some very important but rather tedious people in order to be there. The unspoken threat underlying your attitude is: 'This party better be good.'

---

[1] For a fuller list see the Sprezzatura Enterprises pamphlet: *Two Hundred Christian Names and Their Most Irritating Misspellings*. This publication also includes a short treatise on 'How to Mis-spell or Abbreviate Your Own Christian Name For Maximum Effect'. There is room here for only one example:

If you were christened Kenneth, you may choose to call yourself:

Ken — suggesting solidarity with the proletariat. You are an unpretentious sort of guy.

Kenny — You are a footballer and/or lead guitarist.

Kenn — You are a television researcher. (There may be a hint of sexual ambivalence here.)

Kenith — You are a film director.

Kenilworth (pronounced Kenneth) — You are an aristocrat with Scottish connections.

Kenilworth (pronounced Kenilworth) — You are an aristocrat with Bostonian connections.

Kenneth (pronounced Kenilworth) — You are an aristocrat with Irish connections.

Cernwyth — You are a poet with a hint of ancient mysticism in your penetrating gaze, and no sense of humour.

Xεviθ — you are either an eccentric classicist or a member of the Greek royal family.

Lardass — You are an overweight blues singer for whom any variant of the name Kenneth would be wildly inappropriate.

'What The Hell?'

As it happens the party you've already arranged to go to on the night in question probably won't get going until around one in the morning, so it might be fun to look in on this one first. You'll just drop in unannounced, so if you do turn up 'don't for Heaven's sake make any special fuss . . . I think I've got a vague idea where you live . . . No, don't bother, I'll find it . . . I always say if you can't hear a party from half a mile away, it's probably not worth finding anyway . . .'

Refusing an invitation gives even more scope to the creative sprezzperson. As we saw in chapter 2 Alastair Glass is particularly deadly on the telephone.

Here he is again, sprezzing against J. Philbin:

Philbin   Hello this is Penfold 347.

Glass   I'm sorry you're out. I suppose I'd better leave a message. It's not really important . . .

Philbin   No, I'm here. Who's that?

Glass   Bloody answering machines. Ah well, here goes . . .

Philbin   Hello . . .

Glass   It's just to say I can't get to your little wing-ding on the seventeenth. Sorry about that . . .

Philbin   It's the 16th actually . . .

Glass   CLICK.

Gatecrashing has acquired, over the years, an unfortunate image. Boorish amateurs have removed all subtlety from the practice, and nowadays the preferred term for the purist is 'self-invitation'.

It should be remembered that an actual majority of party-givers make their plans in the expectation that more people will turn up than have been invited. Most of these extra revellers will be friends or partners of bona fide guests, but since they will be strangers to the host, it really wouldn't make much difference if they arrived knowing nobody at all.

The wrong way to gatecrash a party is to sidle in, clutching an apologetic bottle of Hirondelle, muttering vaguely about hoping it was OK to come along.

The right way is to march up to the door and ask to have a word with the host (by name if you know it. Otherwise, 'Could you let them know I'm here?' will have to suffice). Then proceed with confident directness. Shake his hand. Look him up and down appraisingly. Do not smile. If you are acquainted, however remotely, with one of the guests (and if not, how did you find out about the party in the first place?), say in a matter-of-fact tone of voice: 'Look, I wouldn't have called on Susan if I'd known she was planning to come here. But I did feel I ought to spend some time with her. *Particularly at the moment.*' (Here look meaningful.)

Without saying so, you have conveyed the impression that one of his guests is on the verge of cracking up, but fortunately you're here to comfort and understand. Your host will be very grateful.

If you don't know anyone at the party from Adam (perhaps you overheard the address while standing in a bus queue) you will need to be slightly brasher. Something like: 'Isn't Lucy here? Oh my God, she *swore* she'd be at this address after nine o'clock. She actually wrote it down. Good Heavens, you're having a party! Listen, do you know where Dave is? Well might he be coming later? He didn't leave a package for me did he? Oh well, I suppose I'd better wait for him . . .'

The North London Stray Cat Ploy has now fallen into disuse. Essentially this was a gatecrashing technique which consisted in finding some anonymous moggie, tucking it under your arm and turning up at the party with a concerned expression and the line:

'Does this cat belong to you? We found it being sick in our garden over there . . .' (Here wave vaguely.) 'I think it's been eating frogs . . . Oh look, I've obviously picked a bad time. You're in the middle of a party. D'you know, I was only saying to Monica the other day that we ought to have you round to our place. After all, we are neighbours . . .'

The success rate for this gambit was in excess of 70 per cent, but it caught on too quickly. At one party in Swiss Cottage in 1982, the host opened the door to find seven total strangers carrying between them three cats, one of which had been dead for some days, two dogs, a

hibernating tortoise and a plaster gnome. It was the end
of an era.

————The Party Environment————

Nothing is more pathetic than the stage-design of the
average domestic party. The furniture has been pushed
back against the walls. The lights have been fitted with
red or blue bulbs. The kitchen table has been cleared for
drinks and bits of cheese. If it be Hallowe'en there are
dangly black bats. If it's Christmas there are paper
chains. If it's Valentine's Day there may even be pink
cardboard hearts. It won't do. It will not do at all.

If you're having a party, your preparations must be
either nil (see 'Nothing Unusual' above) or total. They
must have impact. Paint everything red, hire an orchestra,
a flock of sheep or a fire-eater, and give everyone a
water-pistol. You get the idea?

Take lighting. A slight dimming of the lights is not
enough. If we're having it dark, let's have it so dark that
the guests are continually crashing into one another as
they grope their way through a black void lit only by the
glow of cigarette ends and the flash of a luminous bow
tie.

If we're having it light, let's have 1,000-watt spotlights
blasting their glare across a dance floor where only those
with flawless complexions and no sweat glands will dare
to venture.

Music must be loud. No, louder than that. Really loud.
There is no point at all in having music as a 'background'.
The purpose of music at a party is to prevent conversation
– even shouted conversation – thereby forcing the guests
either to dance or make love.[1]

This pushing-back-the-furniture business is quite unnecessary. It only creates space, and that's the last thing
you want. Mary Limkin, the well-known Staffordshire
hostess, actually borrows extra furniture and knick-knacks
for her parties, so that all progress of guests from room to
room is halted by interposed sideboards and cabin

---

[1] There is only one other rule about music for parties. Never let
the guests choose the records.

At gay discos it is not sprezzy to intrude upon couples who seem to be deeply involved with each other.

trunks. The house looks full and frantic as soon as the first four visitors have arrived. Her most successful party was given on Boxing Day 1981. She had been to the market and bought a job lot of 182 dishevelled and unsaleable Christmas trees which she stacked to within three feet of the living room ceiling. Guests, as they arrived, were each given a string of tinsel and a pair of rubber gloves and pushed into the prickly undergrowth with the injunction, 'Let's see if we can make it look really festive . . .'

Having settled upon the bold imaginative stroke that will make your party forever memorable (without setting fire to the house, flooding the cellar or giving everyone ptomaine poisoning), you must turn your mind to the subtleties. You will want to give some thought to such questions as: What books do I leave lying about the lavatory? (Plato's *Republic* is good. Verlaine in the original is better. Any pornography should be hard-core.) and: What do I do about 'conversation pieces'?

A lot of nonsense is talked about conversation pieces, especially in advertisements in the Sunday supplements. It is unnecessary, and may be counter-productive, to spend a lot of money on glossy art books, hallmarked silver medallions of Great Insects of the World, or brass cartridge cases inscribed 'From a Grateful Regiment'.[1]

---

[1] George Blossom took the conversation piece to extremes. He made a habit of hunting through biographies of the famous for references to such articles as Churchill's favourite brick-laying trowel, Kitchener's grey worsted golfing socks, the scissors with which Hitler trimmed his moustache, Ezra Pound's bone-handled pickle-fork, etc. Then he would rummage through garage cupboards and kitchen drawers to find reasonable approximations of these articles, which he displayed in a glass case in the dining room. Beside each was a framed photostat of the relevant passage from the book.
He came to grief when he borrowed from the library a biography of Noel Coward, two pages of which were stuck together with what may have been Vaseline. This led him to the mistaken belief that the Master had owned a large brass ostrich. The chimerical nature of Blossom's ostrich (which was made for him at great expense by a student of metalwork at the local technical college) was exposed when Delia Overpond, intrigued by the bird, checked the reference and discovered that it should have been an ashtray.

My friend Wilmot simply places on his coffee-table a single page torn from a recent issue of *Woman's Own*. At the time of writing he is using a page with an advertisement for Mary Baker Sponge-cake Mix on one side, and half a picture-feature about cot quilts on the other. As the eyes of the guest fall upon this unremarkable piece of paper, Wilmot asks: 'Tell me honestly, what do you think of that?'

The conversation may now take either of two courses:

Conversation A

Guest	How d'you mean?: It's a page from a magazine, isn't it?
Wilmot	Yes. What d'you think of it?
Guest	Erm, it's very nice.
Wilmot	Very nice? Very nice? It's the most horrible vulgar thing I've ever seen. That picture! The unctuous prose underneath it! The headline, for God's sake!
Guest	Well, now you mention it . . .
Wilmot	You know, some people don't even notice these things.

Conversation B

Guest	How d'you mean? It's a page from a magazine, isn't it?
Wilmot	Yes. What d'you think of it?
Guest	Not a lot. Typical vulgar commercial rubbish.
Wilmot	I'm talking about the lithography. Where have you ever seen reproduction to that standard in three-colour web-offset out of a British machine?
Guest	Well, now you mention it . . .
Wilmot	You know, some people don't even notice these things.

I have only once known this little routine of Wilmot's to fail, and that was, predictably, when he tried it on Janice Stocking. On that occasion the conversation went like this:

Wilmot	Tell me honestly, what do you think of that?
Stocking	(Studying the page) Hmmm . . .
Wilmot	What do you think of it?
Stocking	It's remarkable isn't it? Quite remarkable. Extraordinary . . .
Wilmot	You see what I'm getting at?
Stocking	Oh absolutely. You know, some people don't even notice these things . . .
Wilmot	I suppose not . . .

After this, Wilmot brooded a great deal, and eventually hit upon the conversational gambit now known as 'Wilmot's Revenge'. It turned upon the fact that Janet is one of those people who speak in superlatives. She is forever gushing about how fascinating, brilliant and beautiful all her friends are. On this occasion she launched as usual:

Stocking	Do you know Edwina? She is absolutely gorgeous. And actually very very intelligent . . .
Wilmot	How do you cope?
Stocking	How d'you mean, how do I cope?
Wilmot	All these beautiful fascinating people . . . How do you *keep your end up*?
Stocking	Oh I don't know . . . I seem to manage . . .
Wilmot	It must be such a strain for you . . . keeping up . . .
Stocking	Well not really . . .
Wilmot	Is it worth it? I sometimes wonder . . .

————Dancing With Dignity————

There are three possible sprezz approaches to the question of dancing. The first is the easiest, and is recommended for the majority of sprezzpersons. It has been memorably defined by O. J. Finch in the formulation: 'Don't.'[1]

Risking the impertinence of expanding on this plangent aphorism, I would add only that the 'wallflower' approach must be a positive act of sprezzatura rather than a mere opting-out. Stand poised at the side of the room, one hand cradling a glass of wine, the other toying ruminatively with an earlobe, and watch the dancing. Wince noticeably at the clumsiness and indignity of what you see. As each couple leaves the dance floor, venture a word of criticism, such as: 'Next time, try rocking sideways on the off-beat', or 'You should use your shoulders more.' And if anyone should invite you to dance,[2] dismiss them lightly but firmly with:

'I should need a good deal more space than this. I'd hate to kick anyone in the head.'

or: 'I like to do a forty-minute warm-up routine before I start. I wouldn't want to keep you waiting that long.'

or even: 'I only dance naked. It feels wrong with clothes on, somehow. Later, perhaps.'[3]

The second approach, known as the 'Bopper', is to dance from the moment you arrive at the party to the moment you leave or go to bed, whichever is the sooner. In fact you should be jigging on the balls of your feet when the host answers the door. Make straight for the music, turn it up loud and start to swing and sway. You don't need fancy footwork. You don't need to be able to click your fingers, execute high-kicks or pirouette. All you need is stamina, a basic sense of rhythm and a certain loose-limbed sinuosity.

The aim is to make everyone else at the party feel they're having less fun than you are. They are standing about flat-footed, exchanging banalities and nibbling

---

[1] Finch's disciple and friend 'Pee-wee' Mason went so far as to add an exclamation mark, thus: 'Don't!'

[2] In itself an indication of sprezz-failure. Go back to the mirror and work harder at your lip-curl. Ask yourself: 'Is my stony stare really stony, or merely pebbly?'

[3] This line sounds better coming from a woman. Why should this be?

In an earnest attempt to improve his free-style disco-dancing technique, Warren Bounce takes lessons from a former member of the Ikettes, under the watchful eyes of his kung fu instructors.

Twiglets, wondering how to break the ice, while you both ignore and shame them.

In time, others will make tentative moves towards joining you on the dance floor. Be the girl who dances with three men at a time (or the man who dances with three girls). Get them doing silly things: lined up doing the can-can, crouched down doing Cossack leg-kicks or bent over backwards in the limbo. Then, when the next slow-to-medium record starts, segué smoothly into an erotic clinch with the one (or two) you had in mind in the first place. Let your sweat beads mingle. Let your pheromones work their sexual magic. Be physical. Say nothing. Use your tongue a lot.

The third approach is strictly for the minority who can dance to exhibition standard. It involves waiting until the floor is reasonably crowded and then moving in and making the others look pathetic.

Good show-off dances to use are the jive, the cha-cha, the tango, intermediate-to-advanced break-dancing (lots of spinning on the crown of the head), and (for women only) the Cairo belly-dance (with or without strip). On the other hand, you should avoid the Travolta disco-strut (too easily parodied), anything quaint (the twist, Irish jig, foxtrot, Charleston, etc.) and anything jolly (the conga, the Birdie dance . . .).

It helps if you can bring your own partner and put on a rehearsed routine, perhaps finishing with the Torvill-and-Dean terminal spin. It need last only three minutes, but you should aim to win a round of spontaneous applause. After you've finished, the only other guests prepared to risk dancing at all should be those who are very drunk.

Sitting on the Floor

The rules which govern sprezz attitudes to dancing apply with equal force, *mutatis mutandis*,[1] to sitting on the floor. The questions to be answered are three: 'When?' 'Where?' and 'How?'

---

[1] If you are looking to this footnote for a translation of one of the commoner sprezz-Latinisms, you should, by this stage, know better.

When?

Do not sit on the floor if anyone else is already doing so, or when the proportion of men with creases in their trousers is less than 50 per cent. At a jeans-and-teeshirts party the move is too unremarkable to be worth making.

Do not sit on the floor if there are no available chairs. It looks like mere inability to stand up.

The party at which sitting on the floor is strongly indicated is the one where such a move will convey a touch of the bohemian, making everyone else feel a bit formal and stuffy.

Where?

Never at the feet of someone with whom you are already engaged in conversation. In those circumstances the gesture implies an acknowledgement of inferior status.

Never in the kitchen or in any out-of-the-way corner. This implies a reluctance to face the limelight. Do it in the most crowded room, and (for preference) in the middle of the floor rather than against a wall.

How?

Never, never cross-legged (too yogic, too sixties). Nor, indeed, with legs outstretched. Sit with your legs curled under you, propped up on one arm, and avoid letting your gaze lift above knee-level. Seem to be waiting patiently for something to happen.

What should happen, of course, is that several of the more insecure and impressionable guests gather round uneasily, then sit down beside you and start to chat.

If, after five minutes, you are still sitting on your own and no one has asked whether you're feeling OK, the move must be judged to have been a failure. Try to work out *why* it failed. Then wait a further ten minutes before putting your head on the floor and feigning deep sleep.

Do not get up.

——Party Food, Drink and Drugs——

There is not space in this brief treatise to go into these matters in the sort of detail that would be required to do them justice. Their social implications are so numerous and significant that a separate work of scholarship, the work of a lifetime, would be needed to explore them fully.

Fortunately, O. J. 'Bull' Finch has left us the fruits of his own research in copious, if stained, manuscript form, and extracts are currently being edited by the indefatigable Mason for publication in three volumes. The first is due to appear in 1989.

Meanwhile, 'Pee-wee' is running a series of weekend training courses on these aspects of sprezzatura.[1] Course One deals with party food, and covers such questions as how to get more than your fair share, and how to get rid of your share if you don't like it. Students are required to memorise Finch's classic table of party foods graded according to their flushability down the average WC.[2]

Course Two, 'Drugs' (Finch and Mason define a 'drug' as 'a chemical substance other than alcohol which is capable of altering the mood or the behaviour of a party'[3]) is already fully booked until Lent '91. The syllabus includes:

How to know all about drugs without being addicted.
Cocaine – God's way of telling you you've got too
    much money.
How not to get busted.
How to get busted with wit and flair.
Learn to dilate your pupils at will.
Advanced syringe-play.
Fifty ways to improvise a tourniquet.

But for the average party-goer, the most valuable course is undoubtedly the third, 'Drinking To Success'. To those of us who had the misfortune to know him, the name Finch is virtually synonymous with alcohol, and the fruits of his lifelong research are of more than passing interest. The syllabus gives only a hint of the course's fascination:

Maximum impact for minimum outlay.
Don't call it home-brew, call it Thunderbird Wine.

---

[1] Admission to these courses is by invitation.
[2] It is worth noting that, on a system which allots 100 points to gherkins and zero to cold chicken with mayonnaise, the average score is only 23. Be warned.
[3] A definition which includes soap powder, correctly used.

Injecting surgical spirit directly into vein (inadvisibility of).

How to cope with a Real Ale Bore.

What to do if you spill your drink (a) over someone else, (b) over yourself, (c) on the carpet, (d) all over everywhere.

Vomiting *a* to *d*.

Be drunk with dignity.

How to make heavy drinkers feel uneasy.

How to make light drinkers feel uneasy.[1]

When to go in the kitchen and make yourself a cup of cocoa.

What to do with the bodies.

The Tea Party

Lord Dacre, in the days when he was plain Hugh Trevor-Roper, developed the technique of offering tea to his guests as follows.

Produce a pot in which you have placed three Earl Grey tea-leaves and a pint of boiling water. After pouring 'tea' for your guests, top up the pot with fresh hot water before pouring your own. Sip the faintly tea-scented water, grimacing slightly at the crudeness of the taste. Don't comment unless anyone is crass enough to remark that the tea isn't very strong, in which case say:

'I would make it stronger for you, but I find it ruins the teapot and then I have to throw the damn thing away. I wouldn't mind, but there are so few of these eighteenth-century pots still around.'

If they ask for milk, sugar or lemon, spend fifteen minutes banging about in the kitchen, opening and shutting cupboards, then return with what they want. Watch in horrified fascination while they drink their tea (which is now cold).

There is a counter to the Trevor-Roper tea-ploy, which can be used as a ploy in its own right whenever you are served a cup of tea. Take from your pocket a half-empty packet of Typhoo and spoon large quantities into your

---

[1] Novices are encouraged to start with teetotaller-baiting and work their way up.

Fifty ways to improvise a tourniquet:
Number 37.

cup, stirring it vigorously. Drink the result without comment.

Glass, for whom this was always too crude a counter, prefers to bring out a thermometer and take the temperature of the tea. When it has cooled to precisely 181 degrees Fahrenheit, and not before, he takes a sip, then leaves the rest of the drink untouched, again without comment.

Only Philbin had the correct response to this one. He walked across to the barometer on the wall, tapped it thoughtfully and said:

'Don't you think, with the air pressure as low as it is today, tea tastes nicer stirred anti-clockwise?

─────────── Party Conversation ───────────

The essence of party conversation, especially dinner party conversation, is wit. There is no substitute for it. Moreover, it is a difficult thing to teach. If you haven't got it, reading this book is unlikely to help. If you have, you need no further instruction in the art of talking at parties.

On the other hand, I suppose it might be useful to give a few hints at this point about how you can contrive to seem wittier than you are. So here are five.

1. Steal

Memorise other people's witty lines and use them. For an average sort of party you will need about half a dozen. A good beginning is Dr Johnson's 'Nothing is more hopeless than a scheme of merriment.' (See page 6 for the rules on attributing quotes.)

Don't steal from recent television programmes or from periodicals less than three years old. The radio is a safer source, but a good deal less tempting.

Don't learn jokes, as such. Joke-telling is profoundly non-sprezz.

Don't preface your stolen remark with a preamble such as, 'That reminds me . . .' or 'The classic comment on sex is . . .'. Just deliver it and sit back with a wry smile.[1]

---

[1] See 'Smiles: Wry, Shy, Dry and Sly.' A Sprezzatura Enterprises video cassette (available Betamax only, natch).

2. It's not what you say, it's the way that you say it

If you are not doing terribly well with the person you're talking to, concentrate instead on impressing someone else. While continuing the conversation, work at seeming fantastic to someone who is almost or entirely out of earshot. Devote your conscious efforts not to what you are saying, but to how you look and sound.

Even if there *isn't* anybody out of earshot, behave as though there were, and as though they were the object of your aim to impress.

The almost magical result will be that you will start to seem wittier than you are actually being.[1]

3. Undermine the opposition

Here are three classic 'spoiling' moves. You will no doubt wish to devise others of your own.

a. When told a joke or anecdote, correct the teller on a point of detail. For example, this is Percy Limboule undermining Magnus Kupferman:

Kupferman	There's the story about Marilyn Monroe. When she was served matzo-ball soup she said, 'I wonder what they do with the rest of the matzo?'
Limboule	Actually the story was that she had this Jewish agent who gave her the stuff every time she went to dinner, and in the end she said, 'Isn't there any other part of the matzo you can eat?' Also it was Mae West.

b. Instil in the speaker a sudden realisation that what they

---

[1] In this connection it is worth mentioning that Sprezzatura Enterprises can supply a set of four audio cassettes for home study:
SE001 – Insouciance. SE002 – Light, dismissive laughter. SE003 – How to patronise without insulting. SE004 – Outrageousness, its uses and limitations.

are telling you is actually in rather bad taste.[1] Thus a line such as, 'Why did the hedgehog cross the road? To show it had guts!' may be greeted with: 'I knew someone who was run over by a lorry. It was awful. They found his eyeballs ten feet away from the body.'

c. Interrupt. Ask for circumstantial detail, the more specific and irrelevant the better. Here is Limboule again, this time sprezzing against Moira Vissell:

Vissell	Do you know the story about Mrs Arnold Bennett going to a party wearing this amazing hat? Sort of a huge jockey-cap with feathers all over it . . .
Limboule	What colour?
Vissell	Erm, red. Or some amazing colour anyway . . .
Limboule	You mean scarlet, or more sort of crimson?
Vissell	I dunno. Let's say crimson . . .
Limboule	The hat or the feathers, or both?
Vissell	Whatever. Anyway, the point is, someone asked her why she was wearing this amazing hat . . .
Limboule	Who?
Vissell	Just someone at the party . . .
Limboule	You mean a friend of hers, or a complete stranger?
Vissell	A friend, I suppose.
Limboule	'Cos if it was a stranger, it'd be a bit of a rude thing to say.
Vissell	Quite. And *she* said: 'It's so that everyone in the room will say . . .'

---

[1] This approach can backfire. A famously diminutive television comedian once interrupted a colleague who was telling spastic jokes, pointing out that, as someone who did a lot of work for the Variety Club, he found such jokes offensive. The joke-teller replied: 'Well you'd better piss off, then. The next one's about midgets.'

Limboule	Where was it, this party?
Vissell	I've no idea. '. . . so that everyone in the room will say, "Who on earth is that woman in the hat?" . . .'
Limboule	. . . Meaning Mrs Bennett.
Vissell	Exactly. And then they would be told: 'That is Mrs Arnold Bennett.'
Limboule	By someone who knew her?
Vissell	Correct.
Limboule	So it wouldn't be *literally* everybody in the room who said, 'Who on earth is that woman in the hat?' because what you've said implies that there was at least one person who knew her, possibly in addition to the friend who asked her about the hat in the first place. Anyway, carry on.
Vissell	That's it. That's the story.
Limboule	So let's get this straight. *Why* was she wearing this crimson jockey cap with feathers, exactly?

4. The absent objective correlative, or 'laughing in the wrong place'

If you display amusement (a suppressed giggle, a snort of derision, a sudden grin . . .) at something which no one else finds funny, you suggest that your quicksilver mind has grasped an unintended irony, a *double entendre* or a revealing admission that has escaped the rest.

The danger of over-using this ploy is obvious. You risk giving the impression that you are somewhat doolally.

If the victim asks what you're grinning at, reply:

'Nothing. Just something you said struck me as funny. I've got this weird sense of humour . . .'

or 'I was just watching the expression on Margaret's face.'

or even 'Please, no . . . (titter) do carry on. It's a serious (splutter) business. Really, I'm all ears . . .'

5. The little-known fact

The difference between a bore and a fascinating talker is often reducible to a single factor: relevance. Both may well tell you things you neither wish nor need to know. But whereas the bore delivers a monologue which cuts across your own utterances, the fascinating talker takes the lightly tossed ball of conversation and runs with it.

This principle applies crucially to the use of the 'Not a lot of people know that' ploy. It is no good stocking your brain with recherché information if you cannot somehow weave it into the tapestry of conversation and tuck in the ends.[1]

For example, Gordon Clapwager is a bore:

Fiona   Try one of the vol au vents. They're scrummy!

Gordon   Thank you. I do think it's a waste serving non-vintage champagne. If you can't afford a Tête de Cuvée you might as well buy Seyssel and have done with it. Most people can't tell the difference.

Fiona   I'm sure you're right. Excuse me.

Whereas Francine Spong has the flexibility of reference that makes for fascination:

Bernard   I'm not sure at the moment whether turn-ups on trousers are fashionable or not.

---

[1] There are a very few facts which actually work *better* in conversation if they are dropped into an inappropriate context without any preamble. Fifty of them have been published by Sprezzatura Enterprises in the pamphlet, *The Truth About Frank Bough and Other Bombshells*. There is space here for only two of them:

The world speed record for masturbating to ejaculation from a flaccid start is ten seconds. It was achieved by a 63-year-old man and witnessed by Wardell Pomeroy.

There is a Finnish nursery rhyme called 'Baa-baa White Lamb'.

Francine   I've no idea. Actually I tend to agree
with Captain Vincent about trousers.

Bernard   Captain . . .?

Francine   Captain H. H. Vincent. Leading British
nudist of the 1920s. He said the
wearing of trousers should be made a
criminal offence.

If you want to leave a party early,
you can always 'suddenly remember'
that you left home without putting the
cat out.

TEST PAPER

Section A

1. You are invited to a party and have decided to invoke Langan's Bluff[1] (the art of being so outrageous that everyone loves you for fear of what might happen if they didn't). Is your opening line:

a. Hello, this is the wife. She goes down on alsatians.

b. Is there a bucket in here? I may want to puke later.

c. Can you zip up me flies for me, darling, I've got me hands full?

2. You are trying to impress with your arcane and colourful slang when a real underworld character walks up and says, 'Don't listen to this guy. He'd piss in your pocket and tell you it's raining.' Do you reply:

a. If brains was bombs, sunbeam, you couldn't blow your nose.

b. 'Scuse me, I want to put the bubble in with this bag of chisels, OK?

c. Why don't you dive off for a nosebag and leave us in peace?

3. When is it OK to sit on the stairs at a party?

a. When queueing for the lavatory.

---

[1] Or, if female, 'Parkin's Bluff'. The opening lines will be broadly similar except that (a) will refer to the husband, perhaps in an agricultural context, and (c) will be an offer rather than a request.

b. When too drunk to stand.

c. Never.

4. During a lull in the conversation, someone suggests, 'How about a party-game?' Do you:

a. Reply witheringly: 'Or why not let's have a go at the *Daily Mirror* crossword?'

b. Produce a revolver and ask, 'Anyone for Russian roulette'?

c. Make everyone put balloons between their legs and oranges under their chins, then say, 'I've forgotten the exact rules, but it's some kind of race . . .'?

5. When you introduce Frances to Kevin, and Kevin immediately corrects you by saying, 'My name's Keith actually,' do you reply:

a. Ha ha. I fell for that one last time. You must try it out on Frances. Look here, Frances, ask him what his name is . . . This'll kill you . . . Just say, 'What's your name . . .' (Then melt discreetly into the crowd)

b. I'm sorry, I thought tonight was one of your – you know – *anonymous* nights. No names no pack-drill, know what I mean?

c. It bloody isn't. Keith's that other bloke . . . little feller with the big red . . . oh dear, of course. I'm mixing you up with Kevin!

Section B (Open-ended questions. Be brief)

1. Give six impressive ways of answering the question 'What do you do for a living?' without actually lying.

2. a. When is it OK to suggest 'a bit of a sing-song'?
   b. What should you do if anyone else suggests such a thing?

3. Give three crushing replies to the question: 'You know everybody, don't you?' (Only one of your answers may begin 'Yes, of course, but . . .')

Now check your score

1. Each line individually scores nil. All three within thirty seconds score five.
2. If he's worringly large, none. If not, any. Score five. Failure to check scores nil and a broken leg.
3. *a* – wrong. *b* – wrong. *c* – wrong (but sound advice for the novice. Score five).
4. *a* or *c* scores two. *b*, done convincingly, scores five.
5. *b* scores five for neatness. *c* is too complicated; score one. *a* scores nil (unless you have completed the Sprezzatura Enterprises course which deals with 'melting discreetly into a crowd', in which case score three).

7
THE OTHER LOT

*Never do with your hands what
you could do better with your mouth.*
Cherry Vanilla

The best thing about sprezzatura – and I've been saving this for last, as a reward – is the fact that it is very sexy. Hythe has proved this experimentally. He graded 100 students using the Marjorison and Pidstock system (a checklist of multiple-choice questions designed to place subjects along a graph-curve from 'pretty sprezzless' to 'reasonably sprezzy'[1]) and then sent them all to a residential summer school. On their return he found a strong positive correlation between high sprezz-scores and the incidence of crabs.

If you have mastered the techniques I have outlined so far, your sexual attractiveness will already have sharpened up considerably,[2] but the time has now come to hone it, as it were, to a fine point.

For the male, a reputation as a Casanova is to be avoided. It leads women to fear that you will toy heartlessly with their affections, and they may even suspect you of overcompensating for homosexual inclinations.[3] Sexual success comes most easily, therefore, to the man who seems interested in women without being obsessed by them.

---

[1] The test is notoriously unreliable for the assessment of extreme sprezziness and total sprezzlessness, but works well in the 20 per cent to 80 per cent range.

[2] Please don't write in with details. They become tediously repetitive.

[3] Or an unusually small willie.

'When the ice-maiden shows signs of
fossilising into the virgin spinster, it is
a kindness to have a word with her
and suggest a less frigid pose.'

For the female, on the other hand, there are two sorts of reputation that work well. You may choose to present yourself as the ice-maiden, a challenge to the seductive prowess of the male. For this one, it helps to be young and beautiful. When the ice-maiden shows signs of fossilising into the virgin spinster, it is a kindness to have a word with her and suggest a less frigid pose. Alternatively, it is not necessarily a bad thing for a woman to have a reputation as 'a bit of a goer'. It gains you a better-than-average number of passes, and when you reject a pass it makes the man in question feel his failure more acutely. Few women, however, have what it takes to carry into the sexual arena the full implications of La Rochefoucauld's dictum: 'There are crimes which become innocent and even glorious through their splendour, number and excess' without coming across as a randy old baggage.

There is a theory that sexual attractiveness is related to physical appearance. Beautiful women and handsome men, it is suggested, find it easier to find sexual partners. But there are two pieces of evidence which contradict this. First, the most cursory study of the wedding pictures in any local newspaper or photographer's shop window will demonstrate that most people who succeed in acquiring long-term sexual partners are in fact distressingly ugly. Second, Hollywood films, television dramas and illustrated magazines show us that, conversely, good-looking people find it very difficult to form stable and satisfying relationships. My advice, therefore, is to avoid sexual approaches to, or from, good-looking people.[1]

———— Seductio ad absurdum ————

The sprezz seduction works like judo. The adversary is surprised to be pushed instead of pulled, and can't quite work out how he/she came to be flat on the mat.

The opening line, 'I think we should go to bed together,'

---

[1] There is no evidence, incidentally, that dieting, exercising, working hard at a suntan and squeezing blackheads are more effective ways of increasing sexual attractiveness than an equivalent amount of time and effort spent rehearsing card tricks, learning to cook and practising a dirty laugh.

or any of its many subtle variations, tends to produce the response, 'Oh do you indeed?' Not a good beginning.

But the line, 'It really wouldn't be a good idea for us to go to bed together' (or words to that effect), invites the response, 'Why not?' Dialogue has been opened. You may proceed in any of a number of directions. For example:

'I'm afraid I might get a little bit carried away and lose some of my objectivity about the situation . . .'

or

'I don't . . . I really don't . . . want to *change* you.'

or even

'One of us will probably regret it. If only I could be sure it won't be you!' (Instant response:[1] 'It won't! It won't!')

Let the seductee do the work

Whatever coy reasons for non-consummation are advanced, do not take issue with them. Agree whole-heartedly. Make the thing an insuperable problem. Thus:

She   I'm afraid that if I go to bed with you, you won't respect me.

He   That's the trouble, isn't it? Men can't help despising a girl who hops into bed with all and sundry.

She   I'm not playing hard to get . . .

He   I know. I know. It's just that you have to keep your self-respect. Without that, you've got nothing.

She   That's right. I'm glad you understand.

He   I do. Absolutely.
(Long pause)

She   It's not that I don't want to.

He   I know. But you can't be sure that I won't take you for granted.

She   Oh, it's not that exactly . . .

He   No, really. No need to explain. I understand.

---

[1] In 72 per cent of cases.

She   You wouldn't despise me, would you?

He   Of course not, but that's not the point.

She   Because if you're sure you wouldn't despise me . . .

He   Mm?

She   I'd really . . . quite like to, actually.

Any seduction works in two stages. The first stage is the establishment of a certain intimacy, or rapport. The second involves shifting the discussion gently but firmly in the direction of bed.

The following lines will be found helpful during stage one:

'I'm feeling rather "on" you at the moment . . .'
'Oh? Why?'
'Someone told me something nice you said about me.'
'What?'
'Ah. That'd be telling . . .'

And

'Who's your best friend? I'd like you to introduce us sometime. I think it would be helpful to me to talk to someone who knows you well.'

Moving on to phase two, here are a couple of lines for the male:

'If you're sensitive enough to know what I'm about to ask you . . . then I needn't say it . . . If you're not . . . then I prefer *not* to say it . . .'

(A long intense stare, followed in most cases by the reply: 'The answer's yes.')

'Can we get something out of the way? I'm very attracted to you. I'd like to sleep with you. OK? Now let's discuss something more interesting. Why *do* Americans install their light switches upside down?'

And for the female:

'When I was younger, I was poor and I was ambitious, and I did a lot of things I'm ashamed of. I have to tell you this because I don't want you to be suddenly surprised to see my face in . . . well, let's say an unfamiliar context . . .'

.'I'm told the average young man thinks about sex once every seven minutes. But perhaps you're exceptional?'

(The response will be, 'Yes, of course,' but then, is he to admit to being *more* sex-obsessed than the average, or *less*? Suppose he opts for being *more*:
  'Only once every seven minutes, hm?'
Your put-down/come-on is:
  'No wonder men find it so hard to be spontaneous in bed.'
On the other hand, if he opts for being less sex-mad than the average:
  'Good God, there are more important things in life . . .'
Then you reply:
  'I suppose that's what makes younger men so attractive.')

It goes without saying that overt sexual boasting ('I'm actually pretty terrific in bed . . .') is teeth-grindingly non-sprezz.[1] But sexually *intriguing* remarks can be highly effective:
  'So often my mind and my body are in total disagreement. For example, intellectually I find it possible to be quite objective about you . . .'

Judy Stiggle does terribly well with the line:
  'I'm sorry I keep moving away. I'm having one of my "frigid" days. It's not that I don't want to be touched. It's just that, when I'm in this state, the slightest touch feels unbearably *intimate*.'

————Telepathia Sexualis————

A Sprezzatura Enterprises survey has shown that, among people in the 15 to 35 age group, 60 per cent of men and 72 per cent of women believe in telepathy.
  When the survey is restricted to those who are of above-

---

[1] Percy Limboule (who was christened Norman as a matter of fact) claims great success for the line: 'I'm sorry about this erection. I suppose you have noticed it. So embarrassing! I've had it for days. Can't seem to get rid of it . . .' But Percy's taste in women is notoriously poor, and when he tried the line on Alicia Hoisington we happen to know that she replied, 'What erection?'

Sprezz seduction: a word of advice.
 At an early stage in the relation-ship, it is a good idea to seat yourself beside your intended conquest and place between you a small object such as a book, brief-case or (as here) box of fig biscuits. If your companion moves the article out of harm's way, it is safe to proceed to the next stage of physical intimacy. If not, not.
 (In this instance, Melvyn left the fig biscuits where they were.)

average sexual attractiveness (the ones we're interested
in for present purposes), the percentage believing in
telepathy rises to 74 per cent of men and 82 per cent of
women.[1]

You can use this fact.

Try, for example, the following party approach, devised
originally by Lionel Fusmond for use against an exquisite
creature, at the time unknown to him, who turned out to
be Emily Meede:

> *Lionel* Excuse me. Stop it. Please. It *was* you?
>
> *Emily* Sorry?
>
> *Lionel* You were aware you were doing it:
>
> *Emily* Pardon?
>
> *Lionel* That trick with your mind. You knew you
> were doing it, didn't you?
>
> *Emily* Well, no actually. What trick?
>
> *Lionel* But you're aware of being telepathic,
> presumably?
>
> *Emily* Tele . . .?
>
> *Lionel* A bit of a mind-reader. Knowing what
> people are going to say before they say
> it? That sort of thing?[2]
>
> *Emily* Oh yeah. It happens all the time.
>
> *Lionel* Well, whether you're aware of it or not,
> you're also a very powerful telepathic
> transmitter. It was like your fingers
> reaching into my brain . . . weird
> sensation . . .
>
> *Emily* Erm . . . what was I transmitting?
>
> *Lionel* I don't want to embarrass you but . . .
> well perhaps if I knew you better, we

---

[1] It may also be significant that within the 15 to 25 sexually
attractive subgroup, fewer than 60 per cent of either sex were
able to define the word telepathy, whereas over 70 per cent
of both sexes said they believed in it.

[2] Note that Lionel's first five remarks are questions. This is the
correct number of questions to use in any party-pick-up-from-
cold.

could talk about it. Maybe do some experiments. . . .

We offer the above for what it's worth, but a probable success rate of only 74 per cent (men) and 82 per cent (women) is not really good enough, is it?

After further exhaustive tests, we have therefore developed the following preferred alternative which has the additional merit of flexibility. It can be, according to choice, either put-down or seduction-ploy.

Sprezzperson Do you mind if I try a little experiment with you? I'd like you to tell me your three favourite colours in order of preference.

Victim Erm . . . red . . . yellow . . . green. Is this a game or what?

Sprezzperson No, it's not a game. And your *least* favourite colour?

Victim Erm . . . brown. Or purple? No, brown. I think.

Sprezzperson Fine. Fine. Thank you.

(Sprezzperson moves away, shaking head, pursing lips etc.)

Victim Hang on. What's it all about?

Sprezzperson Oh, it's a variation on the standard Lüscher Colour Test. It's a test psychologists use to identify emotions and moods. Lüscher used a set of eight predetermined colours. I'm trying to develop a more open-ended approach.

Victim How fascinating! What does it tell you about me?

OK. Let us pause at this point. The victim is securely on the hook, waiting to be reeled in and gaffed. The conversation may now proceed in whatever direction suits your purpose.

Suppose, for example, your intention is no more than to instil alarm and despondency:

Sprezzperson I suppose it confirms what I've

always thought about you.

Victim	What? What?
Sprezzperson	Please don't set too much store by this. It's only an experiment.
Victim	But what does it mean?
Sprezzperson	No, I'm sorry. It's not fair on you. You had no idea you were exposing yourself to that extent. Why should you? I really don't want to embarrass you. Let's just say it's rather interesting and leave it at that. OK?
Victim	No but please! I can take it! Tell me!
Sprezzperson	Sorry . . .

On the other hand, suppose your aim is seduction:

Sprezzperson	What does it tell me? Probably more than you'd want me to know.
Victim	What? What?
Sprezzperson	Tell me, when you gave me those colours, in that order . . . were you *consciously* thinking about sex?
Victim	No. I don't think so.
Sprezzperson	And when I say them back to you . . . (Deep husky voice) Red . . . yellow . . . green . . . Doesn't that make you think about sex?
Victim	Well, now you mention it . . .
Sprezzperson	I wonder if you'd give the same answer to anyone, or whether your choice of colours was something to do with me?
Victim	Well it's funny, I was going to put yellow first but then I said red for some reason. . . .
Sprezzperson	(Moving in for the kill) I think we both know what the reason was . . .
Victim	Mmmmm. . . .

The act of approaching and opening dialogue with a prospective conquest is always difficult, because a prompt put-down can leave you looking and feeling foolish.

The sprezzy chat-up line therefore comes in two parts with a break, or caesura, in the middle. If part A seems to go down well, you can then deliver part B. But if part A meets with a frosty glare, or that weary patronising smile which tall women give to short, eager men (and vice versa), you should go immediately to part B version 2, an alternative line that turns what might have been a compliment into what is probably an insult.

For example, the classic line, 'Haven't I seen you on television?' may elicit a batting of the eyelashes and a purred, 'Mm, well . . . possibly,' in which case you may proceed to: 'I can't understand why they haven't used you in period drama. I see you in something by Maugham perhaps, or Noel Coward . . .' But if you get a glance with all the warmth of a policeman's flashlight and a curt, 'You might have,' you may proceed to part B version 2: 'I remember! The shampoo commercial! You're the one with clean hair on one side and dandruff on the other!'

Similarly the part A line, 'I see you as something small and furry', has part B(1) 'a little bunny rabbit' and part B(2) 'a very old sandwich'.

Here is a further selection:

A   You dance like a French girl I used to know.
B(1)   Somehow the French move as though their bodies belong to them.[1]
B(2)   You'd never have known she'd had polio.

A   Are you doing anything tomorrow night?
B(1)   Perhaps you'd like to come to the theatre?

---

[1] A statement of the obvious, delivered in context, can become a compliment, e.g. 'I like to dine with someone who realises food is there to be eaten' or 'I admire a man who uses a car for driving.'

B(2)   George has flogged me a ticket for his godawful amateur dramatics and I can't use it.
A   You look quite different when you smile.
B(1)   The effect is stunning.
B(2)   Have you had something done to your teeth?
A   I'm going to Monte Carlo for a few days.
B(1)   Would you like to come?
B(2)   Will you water my spider plant?
A   Have you had dinner?
B(1)   I know this terrific little Italian place . . .
B(2)   Well have a crisp anyway.
A   Are you here on your own or are you with somebody?
B(1)   Good.
B(2)   Good.

Sprezz in bed

In many ways, sex is like fishing; the bait is the least important consideration. What matters is where you dangle it, when you strike, the size of your hook and how you reel in.[1]

It is possible to improve your sexual technique with practice and skilled tuition, but it is very unsprezzy to try to do so by reading books about it, so for practical purposes we shall assume that your sexual skills are not going to alter significantly. You will continue to be as athletic, as languid or as downright inept as you are now. Don't worry. We can work with that.

What *is* largely a matter of choice is the attitude you display towards your sexual partner. You may be desperately keen, even ardent. You may be merely amenable. You may be emotionally indifferent. It is important to adopt the right attitude to match your sexual technique.

Study the following table:

---

[1] In other ways, sex is not like fishing; entanglements are harder to sort out, and you seldom need a disgorger.

Technique	athletic	inept	languid
Attitude keen	sprezzy	non-sprezzy	sprezzy
amenable	non-sprezzy	sprezzy	sprezzy
indifferent	sprezzy	non-sprezzy	non-sprezzy

Notes

1. Whereas there is general agreement that premature ejaculation is unsprezzy (keen/inept), there is no consensus on the vexed question of whether it is unsprezzy to come first. The test is whether in retrospect your partner feels that you were early or that he/she was late. Don't attempt to hint verbally at the latter explanation. Just smile tolerantly.
2. Faking an orgasm is only sprezzy if you get away with it.
3. Going to sleep *in medias res* is sometimes sprezzy (amenable/languid) but usually not (indifferent/inept; indifferent/languid).

TEST PAPER

Section A

1. In a situation in which you feel that a full-scale grope would not be inappropriate, your partner is reluctant to go beyond a tight-lipped kiss. Is your next move:

a. knee-fondling?

b. throat-licking?

c. going home?

2. At a social gathering, the object of your desires is being chatted up by a stranger and seems to be enjoying it. Do you:

a. Approach the nearest member of the opposite sex and blow in his/her ear?

b. Greet the stranger with 'How are the kids? I hope you've got somebody *reliable* babysitting this time . . .'?

c. Interrupt your loved one with 'I thought you were supposed to be out of the closet these days'?

3. Which of the following compliments will best convey the impression that your partner has been a sexual disappointment?

a. 'That was . . . almost perfect.'

b. 'That was . . . somehow special.'

c. 'That was . . . nice.'

4. Surveys have shown that a substantial minority of women would rather cuddle than make love. Do you find this fact:

a. a challenge?

b. a relief?

c. irrelevant?

5. Which of these locations would you
    choose for a dirty weekend?

a. Brighton

b. Burford

c. Bradford

d. Balmoral

Section B (Open-ended questions)

1. Describe in detail how, on holiday in
    Yugoslavia, you would go about seducing
    a non-English-speaking hotel employee.

2. You are having a pleasant time with a
    new-found companion, and it is tacitly
    understood that you will later be going to
    bed together. How, without sounding
    crass, can you broach the subject of
    contraception?

3. 'Never go to bed with anyone whose
    problems are greater than yours' –
    Discuss.

Now check your score

Section A

1. *a* is optimistic but uncontroversial (score two). *b* is
    unwarranted. *c* is probably your best move, especially
    if graciously handled (score five).
2. *a* is a bit of a gamble (score two). *b* is a good
    aggressive spanner-in-the works ploy (score five). *c* is
    not likely to be forgiven.
3. *a* and *b* score from one to five, depending on tone of
    voice. *c* is a safe three.

4. *a* is evidence of insecurity, especially if you are female. *b* is a mature response, especially if you are male (score two). But *c* is the right answer.
5. Brighton is predictable (nil). Burford is safe (two). Bradford has possibilities. Remember Wuthering Heights? (score three). Balmoral is unbeatable (score ten).

Section B

1. You wouldn't.
2. You can't.
3. No need.

Appendix

Sprezzatura Association
of Great Britain
1985 Awards

First Prize: Awarded to Leslie Panwick for his 'Scratched Car Improvisation'. The citation reads:

Panwick borrowed a new BL Maestro from his workmate Nigel Stipple, to take his tomcat for neutering. Returning the vehicle to Stipple's driveway, he scraped its nearside front door against the gatepost. Stipple was livid.

Panwick made light of the damage, pointing out that with a little sanding and retouching it could be made as good as new. Stipple produced a Black and Decker and a spray-can and angrily told him to get on with it.

Panwick, a man of no technical expertise, was at a loss. He knew with sober certainty that anything he attempted would make matters worse.[1]

When Stipple emerged from the house, half an hour later, he found Panwick polishing an immaculate car door. The damage was utterly undetectable. Stipple was impressed and grateful.

He did not notice that Panwick had backed the car out of the drive and reversed it in again, and that the door he was so smugly buffing was the offside front rather than the nearside.

The following day he complained at work about getting 'another bloody scratch on the new car. Must have happened while I was parked. Still, if it's all that easy to fix, I reckon I'll have a go at this one myself'.

Second Prize: There is no second prize.

---

[1] Zugzwang. See page 52.

The Association invites entries for its 1986 Awards
Competition, the 'Spreggers'.

Nominations from non-members will be considered.

Send name, address and brief citation to:
Sprezzatura Association of Great Britain,
c/o George Allen and Unwin Ltd,
P.O. Box 18,
Park Lane,
Hemel Hempstead,
Herts HP2 4TE.